AN UNEXPECTED LEGACY

WILL YOU BE ABLE TO FIND YOUR WAY OUT OF THIS BOOK?

ESCAPE BOOK

THOMAS LAWRANCE

Original title: Escape Book - An unexpected legacy

©2024, Cactus Editorial, an imprinting of Amazon KDP

ISBN: 9798329559644

Label: Independently published

Author: Thomas Lawrance

All rights reserved. The book may not be reproduced in whole or in part, or incorporated into a computer system, or transmitted in any form or by any means, electronic, mechanical, photocopying, recording or otherwise, without prior written permission from the publisher.

THOMAS LAWRANCE

Welcome to a new experience, where you will enjoy an exciting novel, where at the end of each chapter you will have to solve an enigma that will lead you to the next one.

You will find side quest puzzles that will not be necessary to continue reading the adventure but that will make your journey easier if you manage to solve them.

The time will come when you will have to choose what to do, your decisions will lead you to one point or another.

And of course, you will find "easter eggs" or "hidden tidbits" throughout the adventure. Open your imagination and let your mind run wild.

Very important things to keep in mind in this adventure

This symbol indicates that you **cannot** turn the page. You have reached the end of the chapter. With the information you have been given so far in the whole story you must decipher the page number that follows the adventure.

How do I know I have found the correct page number for the next chapter?

If you think you have the number, go to that page. All the chapters except the first one have this symbol at the beginning and a sentence of the riddle where it comes from.

It is just as important to know where to go, as where not to go. Try not to look inside the book you haven't read yet, it will spoil the experience.

What if I'm stuck on a puzzle and there's no way to solve it? That's OK, that's what **HINTS** are for.

On **page 138** you will find the HINTS section. These are listed with the page where the puzzles are found.

Each puzzle has at least 2 clues, the first one with the letter **A**, and the second one with the letter **B**. Some of them due to their complexity you will find a clue **C**.

¿ What happens if I'm stuck on a puzzle, I've looked at all the clues and I don't know how to solve the puzzle? Well, you definitely have to go to the **SOLUTIONS** part.

On **page 142** you will find the SOLUTIONS section. These are listed with the page where the puzzles are found.

In order to get the most out of your experience we recommend that you do not look at the other solutions as they are very visual and may lose the fun of seeing what is going to happen in the next chapters of the adventure.

Finally, and most importantly, the last pages of the book contain the NOTES section.

These sheets are for you. You will find them starting on page 148. But they are very important because you will be able to write down any detail that seems important to you that you see, read or sense throughout the adventure (it is highly recommended).

And something that is optional but can help you a lot is to have bookmarks handy ready, since you are going to go back and forth in the story, and you may not know what page you have seen or read before.

SUMMARY

DO NOT CONTINUE THE ADVENTURE UNTIL THE RIDDLE IS SOLVED

BEGINNING OF CHAPTER

TRACKS

page 138

SOLUTIONS

page 142

NOTES

page 148

PRÓLOGUE

It is April 5, 2022, on the outskirts of Boston, on a quiet street in the neighborhood of West Roxbury. That's where our ignorant protagonist of all that was to come, David Mur, lives.

David is many things, but not an adventurer, so he spends most of his day at work, translating texts from now extinct languages, and when he gets home his hobby is reading books.

Want to know what's the next book he'll read? Think you can crack the next book on his list?

Come in and find out

Or

https://escaperiddle.com/firstenigma

WARNING: this riddle is optional, the story starts on the next page, but don't you feel like deciphering the first riddle? It's your choice if you decide to enter or not!

A Boring Life

David Mur's morning alarm clock rang relentlessly at 6:30 a.m., as it did every weekday. It was just another morning in his life, a monotonous repetition of all the previous ones. He got up with the same automatic gesture, turned off the alarm and headed for the bathroom. As he looked in the mirror, the white light of the fluorescent bulb illuminated his 47-year-old face, marked by the traces of time and routine. His eyes reflected a mixture of weariness and resignation.

Breakfast consisted of the same old black coffee and lightly burned toast, accompanied by the silence of his apartment. There was no hurry or enthusiasm in his movements; every step was measured by habit.

Walking towards his work, the city streets seemed to blur into an amalgam of colors and sounds that no longer managed to capture his attention. The people around him moved in a constant frenzy, in contrast to their own slowness. David worked as a translator of dead languages, a job that had once seemed exciting and full of possibilities. Now, however, it has become just another piece of his daily routine. He spent his hours in a dimly lit office, surrounded by ancient manuscripts and texts in forgotten languages, translating words that no one else seemed to want to remember.

Food was another mechanical act. A sandwich bought at the same place as always, consumed while his eyes absentmindedly scanned the pages of a book that no longer interested him. The afternoons were a reflection of the mornings: more translations, more silence, more solitude.

When he came home, dinner was between the hum of the television and the echo of his own thoughts. He often wondered what his life would have been like if he had made different choices and pursued those dreams of his youth that now seemed so far away....

Night came and with it the same ritual of getting ready for bed, reading a few pages of a book before turning off the light. In the darkness of his room, he would sink into a dreamless sleep, hoping the dawn sunrise would bring something different, though deep down he knew it would be just another day in his dull life.

"Yes? Who is it?" he asked in a tone that did not hide his annoyance.

"David Mur? I am Marta, your father's assistant," replied a feminine voice, clear and serious. "I'm sorry to be the bearer of bad news..."

David felt a pang in his stomach. He hadn't spoken to his father in months, maybe years. Their relationship had been distant, marked by silences and absences. His father, a world-famous private investigator, had always been more involved in his job than in his family life.

"What happened?" asked David, a sense of dread growing inside him.

"Your father...has passed away, David," Martha said in a trembling voice. "It was sudden. A heart attack."

David was speechless. The news hit him like a blow, leaving him momentarily breathless. His father, the aloof detective, the enigmatic man shrouded in mystery, had died.

"No... it can't be," he muttered, more to himself than to Martha. "How did it happen?"

"I don't have all the details," Martha explained. "But we need you to come to your father's office. There are several matters that require your attention."

The rest of the call was a whirlwind of formalities and details. He barely registered Marta's words. His mind was elsewhere, lost amidst blurry memories of is father, images of a man always busy, always absent.

After hanging up, he sat motionless in the darkness of his living room. The news has shaken the foundations of his routine existence. He felt he had to do something, but he didn't know what.

Finally, he made up his mind. "I need to see his office," he said to himself. "I need to understand what happened to him." He got up, dressed and walked out into the cold night, heading for the place that had been the sanctuary of his father's secrets.

Arriving at the office, he found himself in front of an old building, whose weathered facade seemed to hold stories of a time long forgotten. The rusty sign with the name of his progenitor still hung in the entrance, like a reminder of his heritage. Pushing open the door, he entered a space that was both familiar and strange.

The room was bathed in shadows and with the only rays of light coming from the street. The bookshelves were filled with books, folders and various objects that spoke of a life dedicated to solving mysteries. The desk, covered with papers and notes, appeared to have been abandoned in haste.

As he scanned the office, his gaze stopped on a coded box embedded in the wall. It was an out-of-place object, something he didn't remember seeing before. Next to the box, on the desk, was an open newspaper in the hobby section, with an unfinished Sudoku. Next to it, her beloved collection of 47 hats, each with its own story, hung neatly on the wall.

"What were you doing, Dad?" murmured David, feeling a knot in his stomach. The scene was an enigma in itself, a message his father had left, perhaps, for him.

He picked up the paper, examining the Sudoku. His father had never been a fan of such games. "Is this a clue?" he thought aloud. He looked at the coded box again, wondering what secrets it held.

He looked out of the window that overlooked the inner courtyard where his father lovingly and carefully tended and kept his plants. He was very fond of them.

He spent hours in the office, searching for some additional clue, something that would make sense of his father's sudden death and the legacy of mystery he seemed to have left him. Every object, every book, every piece of paper seemed a fragment of a great enigma that he was meant to solve. But, for now, the answers continued to elude him, hidden in the shadows of his father's past. With a sigh, he put the paper away and decided to take the coded box with him, hoping to decipher its contents later.

When he left the office, night had fallen completely. The cool street air hit his face, taking some of the weight of uncertainty with it. "I have to find out what happened," he said to himself, with renewed determination. His father's death had opened the door to an unknown world, and he knew he could not turn back.

7 − 3 = 4

RIDDLE LIGHT OFF

Secrets Revealed

The locked room had been a challenge for David, not only intellectually, but also emotionally. After decoding the meaning hidden in the symbols under the ultraviolet light, he realized that he had to link two specific words together using the rope. Each movement was mesured, his concentration was focused solely on the task. By passing the string through the holes, he created a physical connection that seemed to activate more than just a mechanism.

With a final click, the door opened again, letting in the light from outside. David, relieved, quickly left the room. Although he had never openly admitted it, the small, and confined spaces made him uncomfortable, a feeling that was exacerbated in the dark and without a source of fresh air.

Back to his father's office, he paused for a moment on the threshold, taking a deep breath. The air of the office, though heavy with dust and memories, was a welcome relief after the oppressiveness of the hidden room. He decided to take a moment to catch his breath so that he could get his heart rate back. He allowed herself a few moments to catch her breath, feeling her heart rate slowly return to normal.

As he recovered, David reflected on his experience. The secret room, with its mechanisms and hidden messages, had been a test of his ingenuity and courage, a challenge left by his father that he had successfully overcome. He felt more connected to him than ever, realizing that each challenge, each enigma, was a form of posthumous communication, a way to teach and guide him even after his death.

With a new sense of determination, he looked around him. He now knew that every object, every book, every note, could contain crucial clues to understanding his father's work. He was determined to keep exploring, to keep connecting the dots and uncovering the secrets his father had left for him.

Taking a last breath of air, he prepared to continue his search. The secret room had been only the beginning, and he knew there were still many mysteries to be solved. With each step he took, each discovery he made, he came to the truth, and to his father.

Still recovering from the experience in the secret room, David found himself looking closely at the paintings that adorned the walls of his father's office. He had always considered his taste in décor to be somewhat eccentric, a reflection of character. Now, however, he saw each object with new eyes, looking for hidden meanings in everything.

His attention was drawn to one of the smaller paintings, which hung slightly tilted in a corner. It was a vivid oil painting and somewhat bizarre in its depiction, clearly out of keeping with the general theme of the office. David moved closer to examine it better. The painting depicted a chaotic, colorful scene that seemed unrelated to the other elements in the room.

Intrigued, he turned to the other paintings. Each was like a window into his father's travels and adventures. There were paintings of pyramids in the blazing sun of Egypt, of icy landscapes in the Nordic countries, of ancient ruins in the United Kingdom, and of vibrant markets in Mexico. Each painting seemed to tell the story of a case his father had worked on, a puzzle solved in some exotic corner of the world.

David realized that these paintings were not mere decorations or travel souvenirs; they were visual records of his father's research. Each contained clues and symbols, some subtly incorporated into the painting, others more obvious. They were stories of mysteries unraveled, of truths discovered in the shadows of the unknown.

As he analyzed the paintings, he began to see emerging patterns. The locations and subjects of the paintings seemed to be connected by a web of conspiracies and intertwined histories. His father had not only been a detective and a scholar, but also a witness to secrets that many would prefer to keep hidden.

Each painting was a piece of a larger puzzle, a chapter in the chronicle of a life dedicated to deciphering the best-kept secrets. Thus, he understood that, to follow her father's path, he would have to immerse himself in these stories, interpret the clues hidden in each painting and understand how each case connected to the next. This discovery not only gave him a new understanding of his father, but also opened a new path in his personal search for answers.

He was engrossed in looking at the paintings depicting his father's adventures and solved cases, when his attention returned to the quirky oil painting that had initially captured his interest. This one particular painting stood out even more now that David had discovered the connection between the other paintings and his father's investigations.

The oil painting showed an unusual image, painted in a style that differed radically from the detailed realism of the other paintings. It was more abstract, almost caricatural, which gave it an air of mystery and surrealism. The scene depicted was curious: a pot, of common appearance, from which emerged a spider with an unusually large and elegant hat. The combination was so unexpected that it seemed almost comical, but sensed that there was something deeper behind this artistic choice.

"What are you trying to tell me with this, Dad?" murmured David, approaching the painting to examine it more closely. The image of the spider in the hat seemed to symbolize something, an enigma hidden behind its fanciful appearance.

He recalled his father's words about how sometimes reality hides in plain sight, disguised in ways that defy conventional understanding. "Is this painting a metaphor, a code, or just a peculiar joke?" wondered David. He began to search the painting for clues, examining every brushstroke, every shadow, every color used.

The realization that this oil painting was a key piece in the puzzle of her father's research settled in his mind. The painting, with its unique style and enigmatic subject matter, was more than a work of art; it was a riddle created by his father, an invitation to look beyond the obvious.

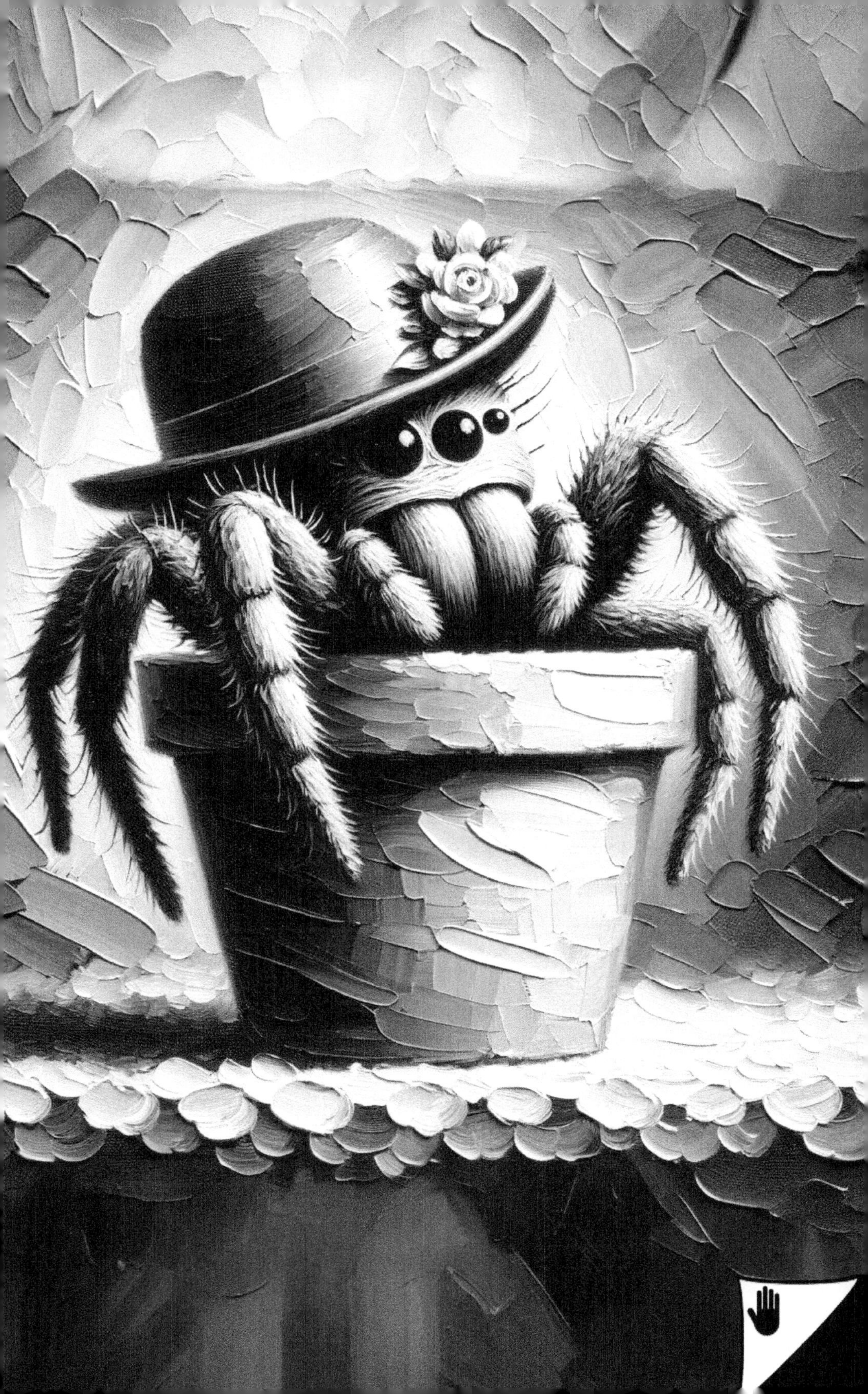

HOTEL CARD RIDDLE

Your Father's Past

David, sitting in the hotel room with his father's diary and the tell-tale letter in front of him, found a detail he had previously overlooked: Dr. Keleby's phone number was written on one of the diary's pages. This finding gave his a new direction in his search for answers. He wondered what role this Dr. Keleby had played in his father's research and what he might know about the Cook treasure mentioned in the letter.

After, he decided it was time to call Dr. Keleby. Although he had his reservations, he knew it was a necessary step in unraveling the mysteries surrounding his father's final days. With the number dialed on his phone, David prepared for the call, mentally rehearsing what he would say and how he would present his connection to the matter.

To his surprise, when he called Dr. Keleby, he seemed to be waiting his call. The conversation was brief; Dr. Keleby proposed to meet the next day in a park near the lake, a peaceful, public place, ideal for a conversation of this nature. The promptness and seriousness in Dr. Keleby's voice left David with a sense of intrigue and unease.

That night, he found himself restless, going over and over the contents of the letter and what he knew so far. The connection between his father and Dr. Keleby, and the mention of Cook's treasure, seemed to be the keys to a larger enigma, something that had led his father to travel to this remote corner of the world. "What discovery was my father so close to making? And what is Dr. Keleby's role in all this?" he wondered.

The possibility that his father was about to unravel a historical mystery, perhaps related to one of history's most famous explorers, was both exciting and overwhelming. David realized that he was about to delve into a part of his father's past that he had never known, a story that could change his perception of the man who had been his guide and role model throughout his life.

With these questions hovering in his mind, he tried to rest, knowing that the meeting with Dr. Keleby might provide the answers he so desperately sought. Closing his eyes, he promised himself that he would follow every clue until he got all the details that would lead him to discover the full story of his father's last adventure.

At sunrise the next day, he made his way to the lakeside park, quiet place of natural beauty. The fresh air and the gentle murmur of the water created a serene atmosphere, but his mind was occupied with the encounter he was about to have. He knew little about Dr. Keleby, only that he was a man of Australian origin and that he had been in touch with his father. This lack of information put him in a position of uncertainty, as if he were playing a real-life version of the "Who's Who?" game.

David walked slowly through the park, observing the people around him. There were families enjoying a sunny day, joggers going about their morning routine, and people alone deep in thought or books. Every man who seemed to fit the description he had of Dr. Keleby captured his attention, making him wonder if it would be him.

He sat on a bench overlooking the lake, his gaze scanning the area, looking for some sign of recognition or some clue that would lead him to Dr. Keleby. "How will I recognize someone I've never seen?" he wondered. He knew Dr. Keleby would be equally on the lookout, searching for a stranger who had answers about a deceased colleague.

Time was passing and he was beginning to feel a mixture of anxiety and impatience. Every potential candidate that passed by him became a cause for speculation. He noticed an older man reading a newspaper, a tourist with an Australian accent talking on the phone, a professor teaching an outdoor class. But none of them appeared to be Dr. Keleby.

Who is Doctor Keleby?

68
27
6
62
44
72
102
92
29
109
12
111
18
19
10
23
79
108
21
28
9
75
98
63
121
37
39
91
55
83

BLACKBOARD GARAGE RIDDLE

Deciphering the Enigma

After long hours poring over the blackboard in the garage, he finally managed to decipher the destination his father had marked out for him: New Zealand. Upon realizing this, he found himself standing in his living room, with the weight of a momentous decision on his shoulders. The revelation had left him in a state of deep reflection, feeling as if he was on the edge of an abyss.

New Zealand, a place that evoked images of remote landscapes and exotic adventures, seemed to be the next piece in the puzzle his father had left for him. However, the idea of embarking on a journey into the unknown filled him with uncertainty. It was an existential dilemma: should he leave his current life, his job and the tranquility of his daily routine to follow in his father's footsteps?

David walked slowly through his house, each room was a reminder of his life up to that moment, a life now altered by his father's history and mysteries. He sat in his favorite armchair, looking out the window, lost in thought. The decision to travel to New Zealand was not just a change of location; it was a step onto an unknown path, a quest that could change him forever.

He remembered his father's stories, tales of distant lands and amazing discoveries. He had always been in awe and curious about those adventures, but now he was faced with the real possibility of living one of his own. "Is this what you wanted, Dad, for me to follow in your footsteps, to discover the secrets you found?" he mused aloud.

Night fell as David continued to ponder his decision. The shadows in the room seemed to dance with his thoughts, each one an echo of the possibilities that lay before him. The choice to follow the mysterious path his father had laid out was daunting, but also exciting. It was an opportunity to discover what had happened to his father.

Finally, after many hours of reflection, David got up from the couch because he had finally came to a decision: he was going to follow the road to New Zealand, to unravel the enigma his father had left behind. It was a leap into the unknown, but also a necessary step to solve the mystery he had begun to unravel. And so, he began to prepare for what would be the most significant journey of his life.

****

The decision to travel to New Zealand had kept him restless throughout the night. He tossed and turned in his bed, caught in a maze of dreams and thoughts about what lay ahead. The image of his father, the mysteries to be discovered, and the possible dangers of the trip were intertwined in his mind, creating a whirlwind of emotions.

In the middle of the night, he woke up startled, covered in cold sweats. A vivid dream about the journey he was about to undertake had shaken him deeply. In it, he saw himself following clues in unfamiliar landscapes, each discovery leading him closer to the truth. The dream, though disturbing, seemed to be a sign, a confirmation that his decision to follow his father's mission was the right path.

Unable to go back to sleep, he got out of bed and turned on his computer. The resolution he had made the night before had strengthened. With a mixture of nervousness and determination, he began searching for flights to New Zealand. He found a flight leaving in a few hours and, without hesitation, made the reservation. It was an impulsive step, but he knew it was the right thing to do.

With his ticket purchased, he started packing. He packed the essentials for the trip, aware that he was carrying not only clothes and personal items, but also the burden of a personal mission full of unknowns. Each item he placed in his suitcase brought him closer to the journey that would change his life.

As he left his home for the airport, he felt a mixture of anxiety and excitement. He was leaving his everyday life behind to enter a world of adventure and unknown discoveries, following in his father's footsteps on a quest that would take him across the world.

The trip to New Zealand was spent in a state of reflection and expectation. David stared out the window of the plane, gazing at the clouds and thinking about what the journey would bring him. Upon landing, he found himself in a country of breathtaking natural beauty, a stark contrast to his usual life.

There he was, in New Zealand, ready to begin a new stage in his quest. Every step he took was a step into the unknown, into the secrets his father had left scattered in a remote corner of the world. With a heart full of questions and the hope of finding answers, David began his journey.

After a long drive, he arrived in Wanaka, a picturesque town in New Zealand that, according to his research, had been one of her father's last known destinations. He drove to the hotel where he knew his father had stayed, a modest but cozy building that seemed to hold stories of countless travelers within its walls.

With a mixture of nervousness and anticipation, David entered the hotel. He didn't go through the front desk; he wanted to avoid attracting attention or raising suspicions about his true purpose there. His intuition told him that the room where his father had stayed might contain vital clues to his investigation.

The hotel was smaller than he had imagined, with a quiet and familiar atmosphere. There were two main corridors leading to the rooms. He decided to take the hallway on the right, guided by a hunch. As he walked slowly, he observed every detail, every door, every room number, looking for something that resonated with the information he had gathered about his father.

As he moved forward, something caught his attention. On one of the doors, almost imperceptible to the naked eye, there was a subtle mark, as if someone had scraped the wood very lightly. To most, this would go unnoticed, but to him, used to looking for the finer details, it looked like a sign.

He paused in front of the door, contemplating the mark. Could that room be the one his father had been? What if that mark was a way of signaling or marking something important? There was no certainty, only conjecture, but every little clue was a thread to pull on in the tangle of mysteries surrounding his father's life.

With his heart pounding, he prepared to investigate further. If that room had been used by his father, it could be the key to unraveling the next chapter in the series of enigmas he was following. Every step he took in the hotel brought him closer to the hidden history his father had left for him in this remote corner of the world.

| 16 | 06 | 68 | 88 | ¿? | 98 |

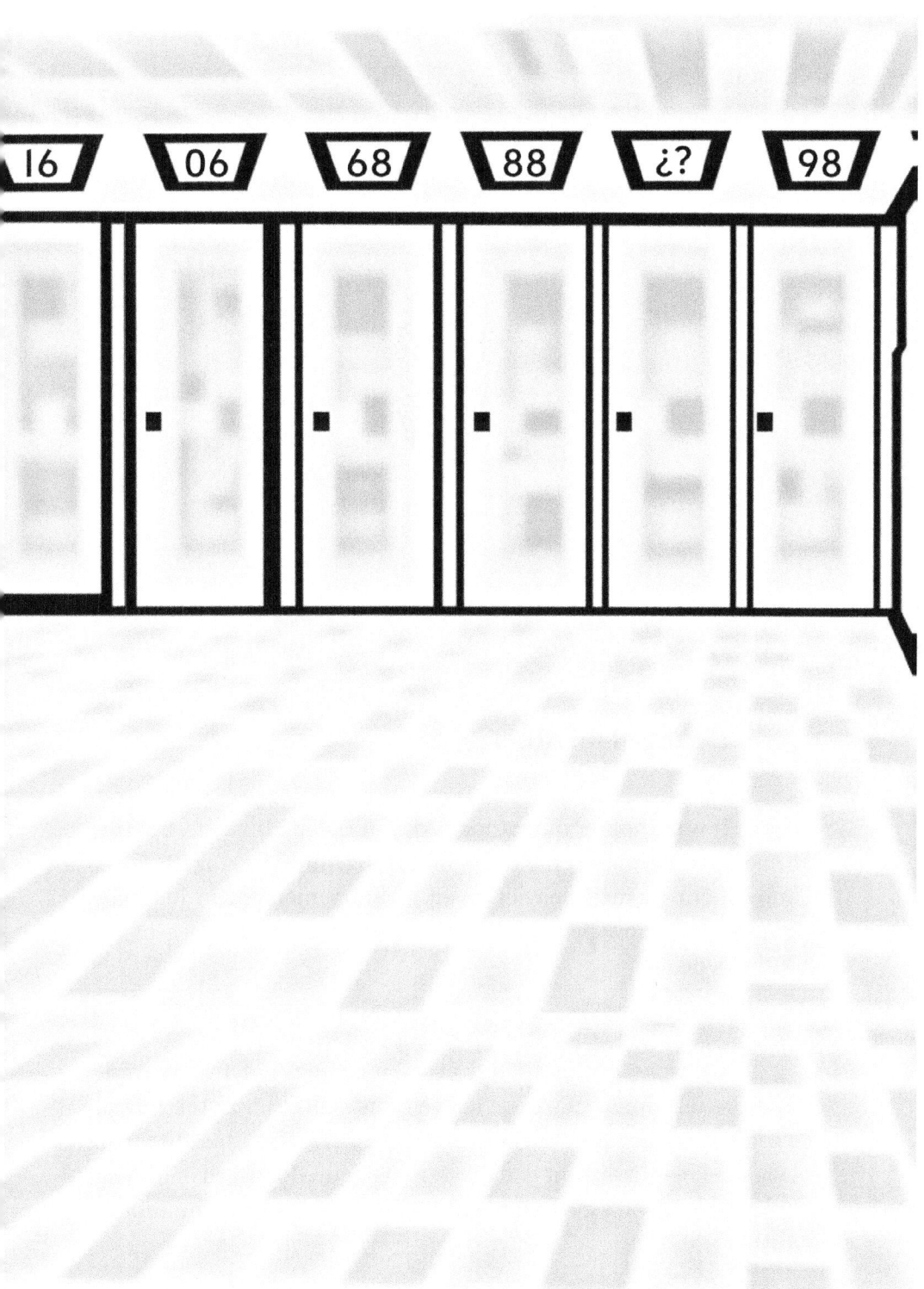

SUDOKU PUZZLE

Death of a Father

It was another monotonous day in David Mur's life, but this time tinged with the gray veil of mourning. Since waking up, every movement seemed heavier, every solitary moment in his daily routine was now permeated with the constant presence of his father's death.

He woke up, as he did every morning, but the morning routine felt different. As he shaved, his reflection in the mirror seemed to carry the weight of a new reality. His father, the man who had been a distant and mysterious figure for much of his life, was gone. David's every thought revolved around this immutable fact.

Work, where he normally found refuge in the translation of ancient languages, offered no solace. He sat at his desk, surrounded by texts and manuscripts, but the words seemed blurry, meaningless. His mind wandered, lost among fragmented memories of his father: a hurried greeting, a distant farewell, the echo of a voice he would never hear again.

The meal was a mechanical act. He ate alone, his mind still tangled in thoughts of his father. Who was really the man behind the detective figure? What secrets had he taken with him to the grave?

When he got home in the evening, he tried to amuse himself by turning on the television, but the images kept flashing past. Every bite of dinner was bland, every minute until bedtime a reminder of the loneliness that now seemed deeper.

David was exhausted and when he lay down in bed, sleep overcame him. The reading of his father's Will was scheduled for the next day. He didn't know what to expect, what secrets or messages the man who had lived among enigmas might have left behind. And as the darkness of night enveloped him, he wondered if he would ever truly understand his father, or if his story would remain shrouded in mystery forever.

****

The arrival of dawn brought no comfort to David. He had spent the sleepless night, turning over in his mind the memories and the few clues he had found in the office. Despite the confusion and grief, he knew he had to face reality: his father was dead, and it was time to say goodbye.

With mechanical movements, he prepared for the day. While he saw her aunt, he meditated internally. "Who am I in all this?" he asked himself. The life he had led until now seemed even emptier in the context of her father's death.

He left his apartment for the funeral, an intimate and somber ceremony. The cold morning only accentuated the feeling of loneliness that gripped him. At the service, there were only a few familiar faces. Most were his father's former colleagues and associates, people with whom David had barely exchanged a word in his life. He listened to their conversations in murmurs, anecdotes and memories of his father, the detective, the man of mystery. He felt more disconnected than ever.

After the funeral, which passed in a haze of formalities and unfamiliar faces, David returned home. He felt overwhelmed by loneliness and the weight of memories, unable to shake off the feeling of unreality that had invaded him since he received the news of his father's death.

Sitting in his living room, surrounded by silence, he found himself unable to perform any task. His gaze was lost in the walls, in the small imperfections he had never noticed. Everything around him seemed to remind him that his life had changed, that the absence of the one he had loved most had left a void impossible to fill.

The hours passed slowly, each tick of the clock echoing in the empty apartment, marking the rhythm of his scattered thoughts. He tried reading, watching television, even cleaning, but nothing could distract him from his own mind.

The will was read first thing in the morning. David knew it was the next step, but he couldn't help but feel a deep uneasiness. What else had his father left him besides riddles and secrets? As night fell over the city, he found himself longing, for the first time in a long time, to discover something new, something that would give meaning to his and his father's life.

When it was finally time for bed, David found himself tossing and turning in bed, tormented by the thought that there was something important he was overlooking, something essential that his father was trying to communicate to him through the objects in his office. The newspaper open by the hobby section, the coded box... all seemed to be part of an encrypted message that he still couldn't decipher.

The next morning, with dark circles under his eyes and his body heavy from lack of sleep, he went to the reading of his father's Will. A place permeated with solemnity and silence. Sitting in an austere room, surrounded by books and legal documents, he felt out of place, a stranger in his father's world.

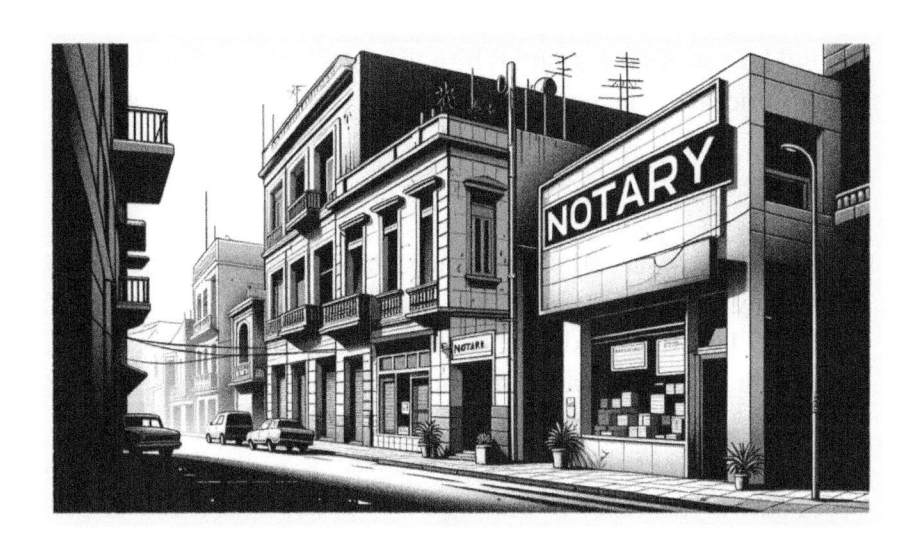

The lawyer, a man with a serious gesture and measured voice, began to read the Will. Most of it was what he expected: legal matters, distribution of assets, and a listing of real estate. But then, the lawyer pulled out a sealed envelope, addressed exclusively to David. "Your father insisted that this must to be delivered to you personally," he said, passing the envelope to him.

With trembling hands, he opened the envelope. Inside, he found a piece of paper with a series of symbols, numbers and letters arranged in a seemingly chaotic manner. There were no instructions, no explanation, just the cryptic message.

"What does this mean?" he muttered to himself. He looked at the lawyer, searching for some clue, but the man simply shrugged his shoulders. It was obvious that the content of the message was unknown to him as well.

David spent the rest of the appointment in a state of confusion. The lawyer's words faded into the background as he tried to decipher the puzzle his father had left him. "Is this a final message? A last will?" he thought.

After the reading, David walked aimlessly through the city streets, the message encoded in his pocket. He felt as if he were carrying with him a fragment of the mystery that had been his father's life, an enigma that it was now up to him to solve.

Arriving at his apartment, he spread the message out on the table, studying it under the light. Hours passed as he tried different ways of interpreting the symbols. But each attempt ended in frustration. The message refused to reveal its secrets.

Finally, exhausted and overwhelmed, he lay back on his couch, closing his eyes. "What did you want to tell me, Dad?" he whispered into the stillness of his home. In his mind, the message mingled with memories, forming a maze of possibilities and unanswered questions. The solution to the coded message seemed as distant as the figure of her father, always shrouded in shadows.

00000000000000000000000000000000000000000000000000000000000000000000000000000000000
00000000000000000000000000000000000000000000000000000000000000000000000000000000000
00000000000000000000000000000000000000000000000000000000000000000000000000000000000
00000000000000000000000000000000000000000000000000000000000000000000000000000000000
00000000000000000000000000000000000000000000000000000000000000000000000000000000000
00000000000000000000000000000000000000000000000000000000000000000000000000000000000
00000000000000000000000000000000000000000000000000000000000000000000000000000000000
00000000000000000000000000000000000000000000000000000000000000000000000000000000000
00000000000000000000000000000000000000000000000000000000000000000000000000000000000
00000000000000000000000000000000000000000000000000000000000000000000000000000000000
00000000000000000000000000000000000000000000000000000000000000000000000000000000000
00000000000000000000000000000000000000000000000000000000000000000000000000000000000
00000000000000000000000000000000000000000000000000000000000000000000000000000000000
00000000000000000000000000000000000000000000000000000000000000000000000000000000000
00000000000000000000000000000000000000000000000000000000000000000000000000000000000
00000000000000000000000000000000000000000000000000000000000000000000000000000000000
00000000000000000000000000000000000000000000000000000000000000000000000000000000000
00000000000000000000000000000000000000000000000000000000000000000000000000000000000
00000000000000000000000000000000000000000000000000000000000000000000000000000000000
00000000000000000000000000000000000000000000000000000000000000000000000000000000000
00000000000000000000000000000000000000000000000000000000000000000000000000000000000
00000000000000000000000000000000000000000000000000000000000000000000000000000000000
00000000000000000000000000000000000000000000000000000000000000000000000000000000000
00000000000000000000000000000000000000000000000000000000000000000000000000000000000
00000000000000000000000000000000000000000000000000000000000000000000000000000000000
00000000000000000000000000000000000000000000000000000000000000000000000000000000000
00000000000000000000000000000000000000000000000000000000000000000000000000000000000
00000000000000000000000000000000000000000000000000000000000000000000000000000000000
00000000000000000000000000000000000000000000000000000000000000000000000004000000000
00000000000000000000000000000000000000000000000000000000000000000000000000000000000
00000000000000000000000000000000000000000000000000000000000000000000000000000000000
00000000000000000000000000000000000000000000000000000000000000000000000000000000000
00000000000000000000000000000000000000000000000000000000000000000000000000000000000
00000000000000000000000000000000000000000000000000000000000000000000000000000000000
00000000000000000000000000000000000000000000000000000000000000000000000000000000000
00000000000000000000000000000000000000000000000000000000000000000000000000000000000
00000000000000000000000000000000000000000000000000000000000000000000000000000000000
00000000000000000000000000000000000000000000000000000000000000000000000000000000000
00000000000000000000000000000000000000000000000000000000000000000000000000000000000
00000000000000000000000000000000000000000000000000000000000000000000000000000000000
00000000000000000000000000000000000000000000000000000000000000000000000000000000000
00000000000000000000000000000000000000000000000000000000000000000000000000000000000
00000000000000000000000000000000000000000000000000000000000000000000000000000000000
00000000000000000000000000000000000000000000000000000000000000000000000000000000000
00000000000000000000000000000000000000000000000000000000000000000000000000000000000
00000000000000000000000000000000000000000000000000000000000000000000000000000000000
00000000000000000000000000000000000000000000000000000000000000000000000000000000000
00000000000000000000000000000000000000000000000000000000000000000000000000000000000
00000000000000000000000000000000000000000000000000000000000000000000000000000000000
00000000000000000000000000000000000000000000000000000000000000000000000000000000000
00000000000000000000000000000000000000000000000000000000000000000000000000000000000
00000000000000000000000000000000000000000000000000000000000000000000000000000000000
00000000000000000000000000000000000000000000000000000000000000000000000000000000000
00000000000000000000000000000000000000000000000000000000000000000000000000000000000
00000000000000000000000000000000000000000000000000000000000000000000000000000000000
00000000000000000000000000000000000000000000000000000000000000000000000000000000000

WHO'S WHO RIDDLE

Doctor's Revelations

Sitting in front of the lake, with the reflection of the water sparkling in the sun, David and Dr. Keleby began their conversation. The doctor, in a serious tone full of respect, revealed to him that he had been working closely with his father on a quest that seemed to be straight out of an adventure novel: that of James Cook's hidden treasure, believed to be hidden somewhere in New Zealand.

Dr. Keleby shared with David how, through a combination of historical research and field work, they had begun to unravel clues that led them to believe they were close to finding the treasure. However, his tone changed to a more somber one as he recalled the day of his father's passing. With obvious regret, Dr. Keleby revealed that he had been with him that fateful day and that, after his unexpected death, he had been the one who had to arrange for the local authorities to take over and subsequently ship the body to his native country.

David listened, absorbed by every word, trying to fit this new information into the puzzle he had been piecing together since the discovery of the diary and letter in the hotel room. His father's death, an event that had rocked his world, now took on a new dimension, shrouded in the mystery of a treasure hunt that seemed too unbelievable to be true, but was real nonetheless.

Dr. Keleby, noting the mixture of surprise and pain in David's eyes, offered his condolences. "Your father was an extraordinary man, dedicated to his quest until the very last moment," he said in a voice full of admiration and sadness. "And he was convinced we were close to discovering something great."

Still processing the revelation, he knew that this conversation was just the beginning. Now, more than ever, he was determined to continue the work his father had left unfinished, to follow the clues to Cook's treasure and uncover the truth behind his father's final days. The decisive entry in this chapter of his life had just been written, and he was ready to read on.

Dr. Keleby, with a look full of memories and a voice imbued with a mixture of respect and sadness, shared with David crucial details about the quest he had been working on with his father. The centerpiece of this quest was an ancient engraving, accompanied by a mysterious talisman, which, according to the doctor, pointed the way to a hidden cave. This cave, they believed, held a long-forgotten treasure, knowledge of which was limited to a select few and hidden in the shadows of the past.

Dr. Keleby explained how the engraving, worn by time and circumstance, had deteriorated to the point of illegibility, an unfortunate twist that had truncated his ability to follow the clues leading to the treasure. However, he held out hope that David's father had managed to decipher and preserve the engraving's indications before its destruction, somehow hiding them in his personal journal.

The doctor regretted not having access to the diary, nor the ability to decipher its contents should he find it. This revelation filled him with a sense of destiny. By a happy coincidence, or perhaps by more than mere chance, he had brought his father's diary with him, carrying it in his backpack as a personal treasure and a connection to his past.

David felt a surge of anticipation and responsibility. The diary he had been studying, which contained not only his father's thoughts and reflections but also, possibly, the secret to finding the Cook treasure had suddenly become an object of immense value and importance. It was a direct link not only to his family's personal history, but also to a historical mystery that could be of great significance.

The sun was shining high in the sky, showing the beginning of what promised to be a day of great discoveries. David, with the journal in his possession and Dr. Keleby at his side, felt ready to unravel the secrets that had remained hidden in its pages. This meeting, in the sunshine of a quiet Wanaka morning, was not just a reunion between two people united by a man who was no more; it was the beginning of a new stage in the search for a treasure lost in time.

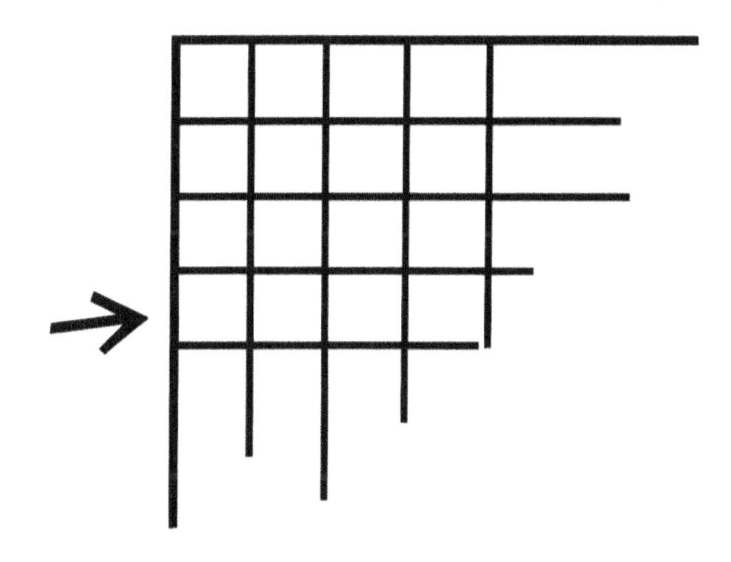

RIDDLE PATTERN ZEROS

The Mysterious Legacy

After hours of concentration and effort, he finally managed to decrypt the hieroglyphic that his father had left him. It was as if the pieces of a complex puzzle had aligned, revealing a hidden message. The message was a letter written by his father, in which he explained that, in the event of his death, David would inherit a number of objects he had collected over the years.

As he pondered the meaning of the letter, he was interrupted by the sound of the doorbell. Opening the door, he found a delivery man holding a large package in his father's name. He signed for it and took the package inside his apartment, feeling a mixture of curiosity and anxiety.

Upon opening the package, he discovered a number of objects that seemed worthless at first glance. As he examined the objects, he remembered how his father loved to tend his plants, spending hours in his small greenhouse, and his fascination with the secrets of the ancient world. These passions, which once seemed distant and unknown to him, now came to life through the objects before him.

David sat in his living room, surrounded by the objects. Each told a story; each was a fragment of his father's past. He wondered what secrets they hid, what stories they had witnessed. In that moment, David realized that, through these objects, he was beginning to understand his father better, to see beyond the detective and discover the man behind the mystery.

David spent the afternoon examining the inherited objects, looking for some connection between them. In his mind, each piece was a fragment of a larger puzzle, a mystery his father had left for him. "There has to be something that ties them together," he thought aloud, his gaze roaming over each object carefully.

After hours of inspection and reflection, he realized that solving the mystery of the objects would require more than simple observation. He needed to immerse himself in his father's world, to understand his passion for secrets and ancient history. "These objects are more than memories, they are clues," he thought.

With renewed determination, he decided that he would investigate each object individually, seeking to understand its origin and meaning. Perhaps, in the process, he would find a way to connect them and discover the message his father had left for him. It was an uncertain path, but it was a path he felt he had to travel, not only to unravel the mystery, but to get closer to the enigmatic figure of his father, the man who had been a mystery in himself.

One of the objects was an old news journal that particularly caught his attention. Then there was an ordinary notebook, with worn leather covers and yellowed pages. But, upon opening it, David discovered that all the pages were empty, except for the first page, which showed a series of torn holes. "How strange," he muttered, feeling a mixture of curiosity and frustration.

NEW YORK TIMES

Six November 2011

Scientific Discovery Revolutionizes Sustainable Energy

Research team announces breakthrough in solar technology with 92% efficiency

November 6, 2011, New York - A team of scientists at Columbia University has made a groundbreaking discovery in solar panel technology, achieving a record 92% efficiency. This breakthrough promises to significantly reduce solar energy costs for more than 50 million homes in the United States.

The team, led by Dr. Elizabeth Huang, has worked for 11 years and four months on this project, overcoming technical hurdles that for decades limited peak efficiency to 70%. This achievement is a major step toward a greener, more sustainable future

Circus Brings Magic to the City

After a long wait, the acclaimed Circo Estelar returns to enchant the city with its tent of wonders. From October 30, world-famous artists and amazing acts will be delighting young and old alike. With acts ranging from trapeze artists to magicians, the circus promises an unforgettable experience. Tickets are now available for this limited season.

don't miss out!

SUCCESS

Once upon a time there was a bald man, named Roberto, who had a peculiar plaster cat named Pedrín. Every afternoon, Roberto would walk Pedrín around the park, combing his non-existent fur with a golden comb. One day, Roberto couldn't find his precious comb, "How will I comb Pedrín's hair now?" he wondered as he frantically searched. In an act of comic desperation, he began to use the comb on his own bald head, hoping for a miracle. Seeing no results, he let out a laugh and decided it was time to innovate. He picked up a feather and began to "stroke" Pedrín with it. Passersby laughed at the sight of the bald man and his plaster cat enjoying their evening stroll, proving that sometimes happiness is in the simplest things.

MONOLITH RIDDLE

The Complete Legacy

He stood in front of the enigmatic monolith; he concentrated on the inscriptions there. Remembering the patterns and symbols he had sketched in his notebook, he adjusted a carved bone fragment he had found nearby, carefully placing it in a specific crevice of the monolith. To his surprise, the monolith responded as if it were part of an ancient but perfectly preserved mechanism.

Unexpectedly, with a smooth and precise movement, the monolith began to move backwards, revealing a hole hidden in the ground, somewhat larger than a barrel. He watched in amazement as the entrance to a secret grotto, hidden for years by dense vegetation and the mysteries of time, opened before him.

Nothing could prevent a chill from running through his entire body. The discovery of the grotto filled him with a mixture of excitement and awe. He was at a crucial point in his adventure, on the brink of exploring the unknown, literally following in his father's footsteps in a quest that had transcended merely being a translator of dead languages. However, the thought of delving into the dark, unknown grotto made him hesitate. "What secrets does this place hide? What did my father find here?" he wondered.

David was tired of the long journey, coupled with indecision and fear of the unknown, weighed on him. He was exhausted, both physically and emotionally. "This goes beyond translating ancient texts. This is what my father lived, what consumed him," David reflected, sensing the enormous distance between his daily life and that of the researcher who had been his father.

Rather ahead of him lay a grotto with its dark and seemingly deep entrance, representing a threshold to a world he had never imagined exploring. He was at a crossroads between the desire to continue the search for his father and the safer option of returning to his normal life.

"Exactly, how far am I willing to go?" he questioned, staring at the dark hole in the floor. Curiosity and the need for answers fought against the instinct for self-preservation. At that moment, he understood that this quest was more than solving a mystery; it was a journey into the deepest part of himself and into the legacy his father had left him.

David, with his heart beating faster and faster, he took a deep breath and made a decision. With a mixture of fear and determination, he prepared to descend into the grotto, determined to face whatever it was that lurked within. It was a step into the unknown, but also towards understanding his father and the mission he had entrusted to him.

- "Come on David", he thought internally- . After a pause of contemplation and a deep breath, David summoned the courage to face the unknown. He turned on his flashlight, casting a beam of light into the dark depths of the hole that opened before him. The light revealed that the drop was approximately two meters, a considerable distance, but not insurmountable.

Once at that point, he reached for a sizable rock and threw it into the grotto. The dull sound of the rock hitting the bottom provided him with a small reassurance: he would now have a foothold to facilitate his exit. After making sure everything was ready, he carefully slid down the hole, leaning on the rock he had previously thrown.

In this moment, nothing good was going through his mind at that moment. What did he expect to be in there? In the grotto he found a damp, cool atmosphere, a stark contrast to the warm, dry air of the forest outside. The lantern illuminated the walls of the grotto, revealing a rudimentary but deliberate construction. It was evident that someone had excavated and shaped this space, perhaps many years ago. The walls, floor and ceiling showed signs of having been worked with basic tools, giving the grotto a sense of being a place deliberately created for a specific purpose.

Now David moved slowly, inspecting the area with his flashlight. Every inch of the interior seemed to have a story to tell, a fragment of the past that was waiting to be discovered. The idea that he was stepping into a place his father had explored generated a deep connection with him, as if across time and space, they were sharing the same experience.

The dampness of the place was palpable, and the air had an earthy smell, mixed with the scent of antiquity. As he went on, he realized that this grotto was more than just a shelter or hiding place; he had a sense of being in a place that had witnessed significant events, perhaps even related to the Cook treasure his father had been searching for.

With each step, he was drawn deeper into the mystery, feeling he was on the verge of discovering something momentous. The grotto, with its rudimentary construction and air of long-kept secrets, seemed to be the final piece of the puzzle, the final connection in the search for his father's legacy. Cautiously, but with a growing sense of anticipation, he continued his exploration, ready to confront whatever was waiting to be discovered in the shadows of history.

As he cautiously advanced through the grotto, a sudden vibration in his backpack caused him to stop. Startled, he opened the backpack to investigate the source of the unexpected movement. Exploring its contents, he discovered that the talisman he had found next to his father's diary was the source of the vibration. The object, which until that moment had remained inert, seemed to have been activated by some unknown force, as if the grotto itself had awakened a latent energy within it.

Intrigued and cautious, he pulled the talisman out of the backpack. Holding it in his hand, he felt a palpable connection to the object; it vibrated gently, resonating with a power that seemed ancient and mysterious. "What secrets do you keep?" he murmured, examining the amulet with a mixture of awe and respect.

At that moment, he remembered his father's diary. With the talisman still in one hand, he pulled out the journal with the other and opened it to the pages where the blurred map was. By the light of his flashlight, David began to see the map in a new light. The outlines and markings, which had seemed confusing and unclear before, now took on new meaning in the presence of the vibrating talisman. "Are you showing me the way?" he wondered aloud, as the puzzle piece began to fit together in his mind.

Upon closer examination of the talisman, he noticed something he had not seen before: a small writing had appeared on the surface of the amulet, as if it had been revealed when activated by the energy of the grotto. The words, engraved in an ancient script, appeared to be a key or an addition to the information in the diary.

David immersed himself in the task of deciphering the message, comparing it to the map in the diary. With each word he managed to interpret, he felt he was getting closer to solving the mystery that had brought his father to this remote part of the world. The grotto, with its ancient walls and air of unrevealed secrets, was the perfect setting for this moment of discovery.

"I'm close, very close," he thought, feeling a surge of excitement and determination. The talisman, now active and vibrant in his hand, was the key that unlocked the secrets of the past, guiding him toward the path his father had so passionately pursued. With the journal and the talisman as his guides, he continued his exploration of the grotto, each step bringing him closer to the heart of the mystery that had defined his father's legacy.

Does the talisman seem to be teaching you something?

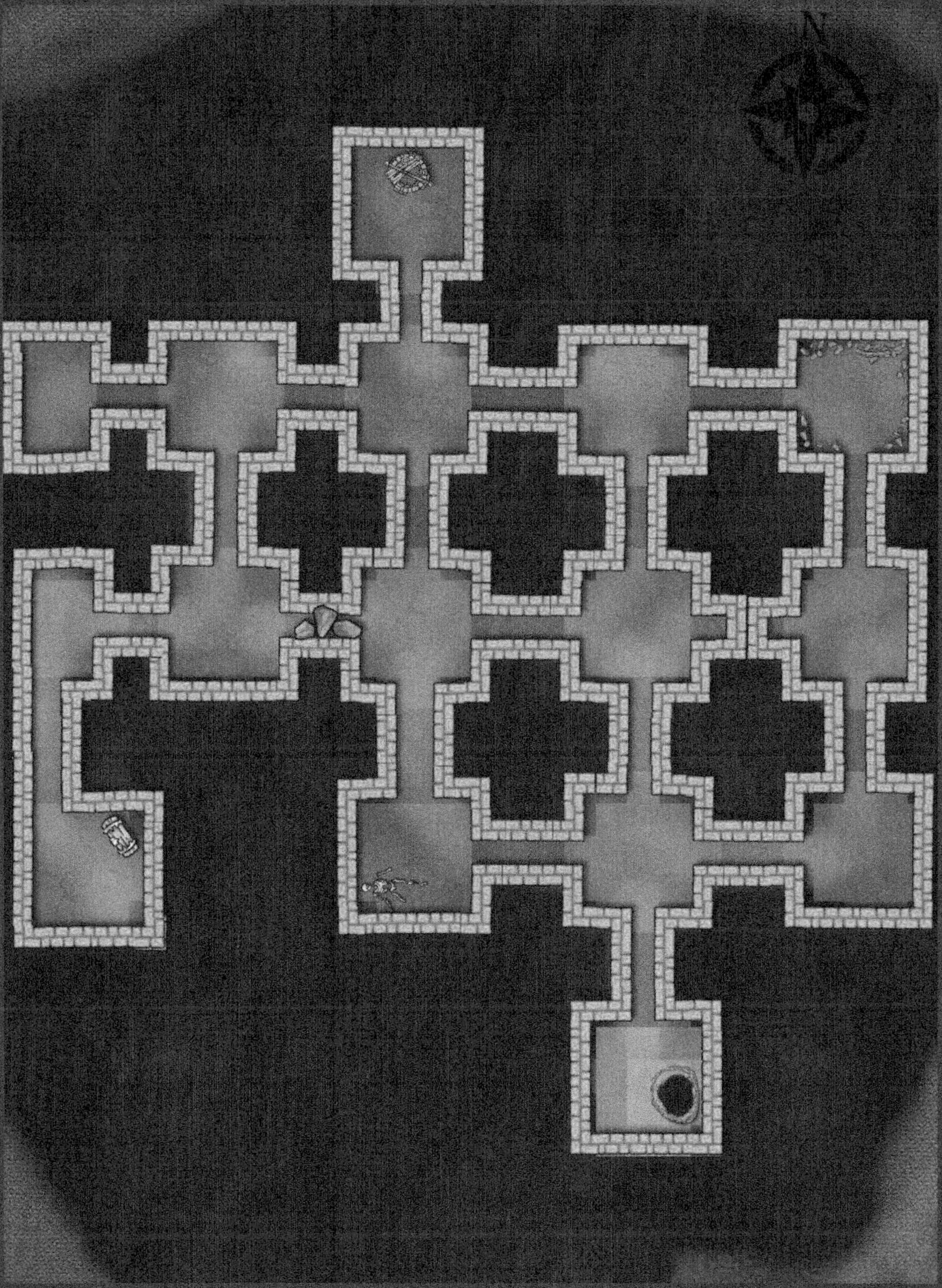

RIDDLE HOLES DAILY

An Unexpected Message

David was in his study, surrounded by his inherited objects, when he understood that these holes in the diary solved the problem by putting it on top of his letter.

Suddenly, the encrypted message caught his attention. Among the jumble of numbers and letters, a few words stood out: "**55 SPIDERS**".

They repeated in his mind, an echo with no apparent meaning. "What could you be trying to tell me, Dad?" he murmured, feeling confusion intertwine with curiosity.

****

A few days later, his reflection was interrupted by the arrival of the letter carrier, who handed him a worn and yellowed postcard. Seeing the familiar handwriting, he immediately recognized his father's handwriting. The postcard, dated 14 days earlier, showed a blurred image of a distant and exotic landscape.

He flipped the card over and read the hastily written words: "David, be careful. You are in danger. There are things you do not yet understand. Trust no one." The message was short, but charged with a palpable urgency. He felt a shiver run down his spine. "In danger? What are you talking about, Dad?"

The postcard offered no further clues, only the warning and a growing sense of paranoia. He wandered around his apartment, examining each object his father had left him, wondering if among them was hidden the key to understanding the warning.

He looked out the window, watching the people on the street. The normality of the scene contrasted with the turbulence of his thoughts. "What dangers, and what do the 55 spiders have to do with any of this?" questions swirled in his mind, but the answers seemed farther away than ever.

With the postcard in hand, David knew there was something bigger at stake, something his father had started and now he had to continue. The sense of danger made him hesitate, but the need for answers pushed him forward. "I have to find out, for you, Dad," he said to himself, sensing a new purpose in his quest. The postcard wasn't just a warning; it was a call to unravel the secrets his father had left behind.

As the days passed, he began to feel the weight of a hidden truth, a shadow lengthening over his daily life. The warning on the postcard, "be careful, you are in danger," echoed in his mind at every turn. He began to look around with a mixture of suspicion and caution, wondering if anyone else was aware of the secrets his father had left him.

"What did you discover, Dad, that could put me in danger?" wondered David, going over and over the objects and the postcard. Each object seemed to have its own story, each a fragment of a larger puzzle his father had been piecing together. But what picture did they form together?

In his apartment, surrounded by his father's enigmas, he began to feel like the protagonist of one of the detective stories his father loved so much. However, this was not fiction; it was his life, and the stakes were real.

The nights became long for David, filled with research and speculation. He began to draw connections between the objects, the warning on the postcard, and the few memories he had of conversations with his father. "Were you investigating something dangerous, something that now endangers me?" he questioned.

He was examining again the deteriorated postcard he had received, trying to find some detail he had overlooked. The blurry image of the landscape didn't tell him much, but there was something about the way his father had written the note that made him think there was more to it than met the eye.

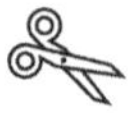

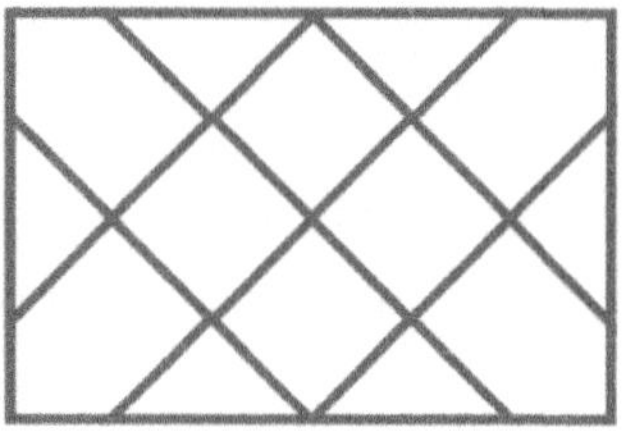

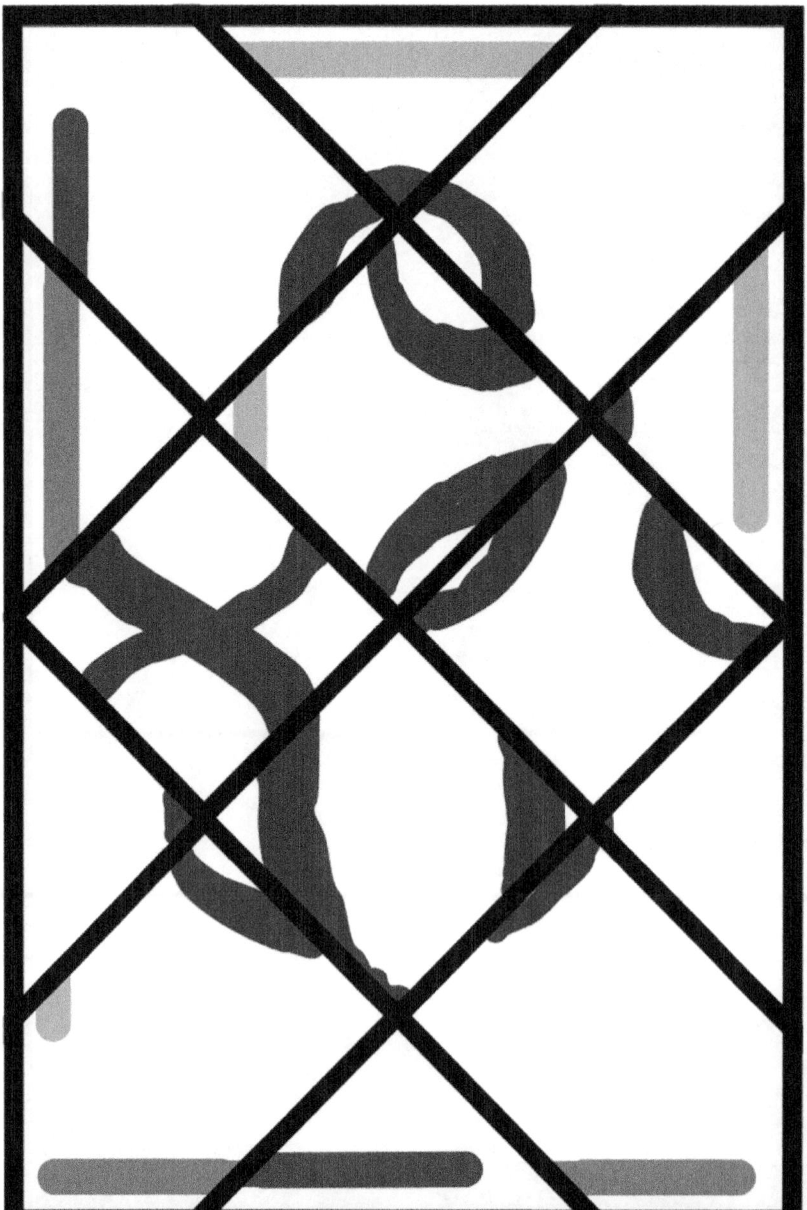

RIDDLE ROAD SYMBOLS

Path to Truth

After his revealing conversation with Dr. Keleby, David found himself with a new determination. As he studied his father's journal further, he discovered what appeared to be a detailed trail, a series of clues and coordinates meticulously noted between the pages. Each clue solved not only brought him closer to Cook's treasure, but also led to new mysteries, each more intriguing than the last.

With the road mapped out in the journal as his guide, he rented a 4x4 car, ideal for the challenging terrain he would have to traverse. The journey took him through spectacular scenery, crossing rugged mountains, skirting crystal-clear lakes and crossing rushing rivers. New Zealand's wilderness was on full display, offering breathtaking views and reminding him of the magnitude of his adventure.

As he followed the diary's directions, he plunged deeper into the heart of the country. The road became increasingly challenging, testing his determination and his ability to follow his father's enigmatic instructions. Every kilometer he traveled was another step closer to solving the mystery that had consumed him father's last days.

Finally, he reached a densely wooded area where the road became impassable for the vehicle. David stopped the SUV and prepared to continue by foot. Despite the fatigue, his spirit was filled with renewed energy. The proximity of the final destination gave him strength; he felt he was about to discover something glorious.

Equipped with the essentials and with the journal securely fastened in his pack, he set off into the forest. The vegetation was thick, and the terrain uneven, but he was determined to go all the way. Each step brought him closer to the place marked in the journal, to the place that, he hoped, would reveal to him the secrets his father had so passionately pursued.

The investigation of the truth, which had begun in his father's office and had taken him across oceans and continents, was reaching its climax in that remote corner of New Zealand. With his heart full of questions and hope for answers, David went on his way through the forest, toward a destination that promised to reveal more than he had ever imagined.

The forest grew thicker and thicker as he walked on, entering a world where sunlight struggled to filter through the thick canopy of leaves. The path, barely visible, led him through a natural maze of trees and undergrowth, in an environment that seemed untouched by man in years.

As he walked, he began to feel a growing uncertainty. The density of the forest and the uniformity of the landscape made him doubt whether he was following the right path. "Am I lost or, am I going around in circles?" he wondered, as he checked his father's journal for any clues that would confirm his route.

In those moments of isolation, David's thoughts became entangled with conspiracy theories and occult stories. He recalled his father's notes about Cook's treasure and discussions with Dr. Keleby. "Why was this treasure so important to you, Dad?" he mused. The possibilities were so many: a priceless historical relic, a well-kept secret that could change history, or simply the latest obsession of a man dedicated to deciphering the mysteries of the past?

The forest air was charged with a deep silence, broken only by the crunching of leaves under their feet and the recognizable song of a native bird called Tui. David continued to move forward, guided by a mixture of intuition and the sparse indications in his father's journal. With each step, the feeling of being close to something significant grew within him.

The forest, with its wild and untamed beauty, seemed like a guardian of time, hiding secrets that only the most daring or the most desperate would attempt to uncover. For him, every tree, every shadow, every whisper of the wind became a witness to his quest for truth, a quest that had begun as an attempt to understand his father, but had now become an essential part of his own story.

With renewed determination, David pressed on, moving deeper into the heart of the forest, toward an unknown destination, but one he felt ever closer. His father's story, intertwined with riddles and theories beyond imagination, was leading him down a path he would never have expected to travel.

He kept pushing through the dense vegetation that closed in his path. The sound of his own movements mingled with the murmur of the wind through the trees, creating a natural symphony that accompanied him on his lonely journey. "I must be close, right, Dad?" he murmured to himself, as he pushed aside branches and ferns.

Suddenly, in the middle of the thicket, his eyes came across a structure that seemed out of place, a stone monolith standing imposingly among the trees. Startled, he stopped and approached cautiously. "What are you doing here, in the middle of nowhere?" he wondered aloud, as he began to push aside the vegetation that covered part of the monolith.

As he removed the ferns and vines, David discovered inscriptions on the stone. The letters and symbols etched into the surface were enigmatic, unlike anything he had ever seen before.

As he ran his fingers over the engravings, trying to decipher their meaning, he realized that they did not fit the expectations he had formed in his mind. "This... this doesn't make sense," he commented, frowning in confusion.

The monolith, with its mysterious inscriptions, seemed to be one more piece of the puzzle David was trying to solve. "Were you part of what my father was looking for?" he wondered, as he examined every detail of the stone. The inscriptions could be clues, possibly related to Cook's treasure, or perhaps directions to an even more secret location.

He took out his notebook and began sketching the monolith and its engravings, knowing that every detail could be crucial. He felt like an explorer of ancient times, discovering a lost artifact deep in an unexplored forest.

As darkness fell, the shadows of the forest lengthened, giving the monolith an even more mysterious appearance. He knew he must return soon, but he promised himself that he would return, equipped with more tools and knowledge to decipher the secrets the monolith held.

"What mystery does this monolith hide?" murmured David. In this enigmatic puzzle, something didn't fit, something was out of place. The tiny pieces were movable, stacked with precision, concealed a secret waiting to be discovered.

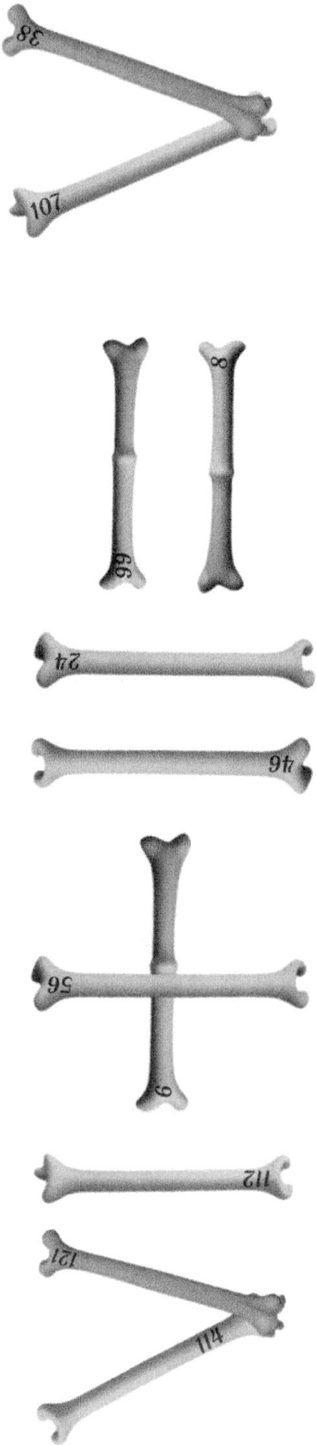
38
107
8
69
24
46
56
6
112
121
114

IT APPEARS TO ONLY LET ONE BONE MOVE.

IF YOU MOVE MORE THAN ONE IT WILL BE BLOCKED!

RIDDLE ENCRYPTED BOX

BONUS

David, with a satisfied smile on his face, congratulated himself. The feeling of having found an additional clue to his adventure was exhilarating. The box, which looked like a simple collection of souvenirs, thanks to the list of pots and the image of the inner courtyard, he had managed to open.

As he went through the contents of the box, his attention was drawn to an antique but well-preserved ultraviolet light lantern. "This might come in handy," he thought, deciding to carry it with him always, as a symbol of light in his quest for occult knowledge. The lantern, with its sturdy design and aura of past histories, seemed to be more than just an object; it was a companion on his journey.

In addition, he found several travel notebooks belonging to his father. They were old, with covers worn by time and pages full of notes and sketches. One of the notebooks contained detailed accounts of an expedition to the Nordic countries, with descriptions of northern lights, eternal ice and Viking legends.

The other notebook was a fascinating account of a journey through the oldest civilizations of the Americas, with observations of Mayan and Aztec ruins, as well as reflections on the cultures and traditions of indigenous peoples.

He flipped through the pages, marveling at his father's stories, feeling closer to him than ever. Each notebook was a treasure trove of knowledge and adventure, a legacy of discoveries and experiences that he now had the honor of continuing. These notebooks not only offered him insight into his father's past, but also provided inspiration and guidance for his own adventure.

Now go back to the point in the story where you left off.

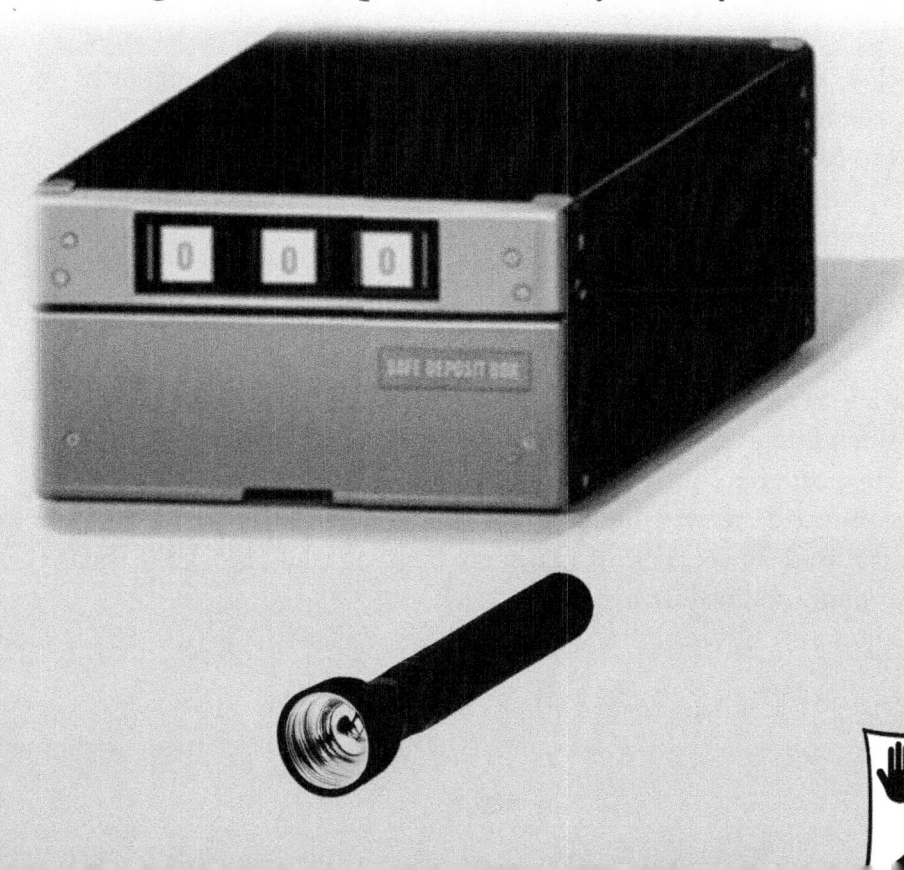

PUZZLE POSTAL RIDDLE

The Secret Office

David, with the newly discovered information, understood that the secret location mentioned in his father's enigmatic messages was, surprisingly, in his own city. He wasted no time; the feeling that every second was crucial drove him. He left his apartment, carrying with him the mixture of fear and excitement that had been growing inside him.

He arrived at the address indicated, an old building that had no signage or any indication of what it housed. The time-worn facade concealed the secrets David was eager to discover. He peered through a dusty window and saw something that confirmed he was in the right place: a photo of his father, captured during one of his many trips around the world, sat proudly on the desk inside.

However, the door was locked and there was no sign that anyone had entered or left recently. Driven by a mixture of desperation and a need to uncover the mystery, David made a drastic decision. He looked around to make sure no one was watching him and, with a blunt object he found nearby, he smashed the glass of the door. Once inside, he found himself in what had been his father's personal and professional refuge.

The office was a space steeped in history and mystery. Shelves full of books, scattered documents, old maps and handwritten notes filled the room. It was like stepping into his father's mind, a place where every object, every book, every handwritten note could be the key to discovering what David so desperately needed to understand.

With deep respect, he began to explore the office. Each book he pulled from the shelves seemed to tell a story of its own, each document seemed to be a piece of a great puzzle that his father had devoted his life to putting together. "What were you looking for here, Dad?" wondered David as he examined them.

Time seemed to stand still as he immersed himself in his father's world. Each discovery gave him a new understanding, not only of his father's research, but also of the man himself. This office, this sanctuary of knowledge and curiosity, was a testament to his father's legacy, and David felt closer to him than ever.

Lost in thoughts and memories, he knew that every clue, every fragment of information he found there, would bring him one step closer to deciphering the mystery his father had left behind.

As he continued his meticulous exploration of the office, one object in particular caught his attention. Among piles of papers and old books, he found a worn and carefully folded map. He spread it out on the desk, revealing a series of handwritten marks and notes. They were key locations, meticulously marked, that his father had researched over the years. Each mark on the map seemed to tell a story, each side note suggested a hidden clue or an important discovery.

However, despite the intriguing nature of the map, David felt an even greater attraction to the bookshelf full of books lining one wall of the office. There was something about those books, about their arrangement and the wear and tear on their spines, that called to him with an urgency he couldn't explain. "Books first," he said to himself, setting the map aside to review later.

He approached the bookshelf. There was a fascinating mix of ancient and modern works, some in languages he recognized and some in languages he had never seen. Each book seemed to have been selected for a specific purpose, as if his father had been collecting pieces for an intellectual puzzle.

He began to realize that his father was not just a detective in the conventional sense; he was a scholar, a seeker of hidden truths in history and mythology. "What were you trying to find,

Dad?" he murmured as he read fragments of texts about ancient civilizations, archaeological theories and forgotten myths.

Each book he reviewed added another layer of mystery and admiration for his father. It was clear that the books were a crucial part of his father's research, and he was determined to discover the link between them and the other objects in the office, including the map he had set aside. This was a journey through his father's mind, a journey that David knew was essential to unlock the secrets he had inherited.

He focused on the bookshelf behind his progenitor's desk, there were all kinds of books, but he began to see a pattern that something didn't add up, something that seemed out of the ordinary.

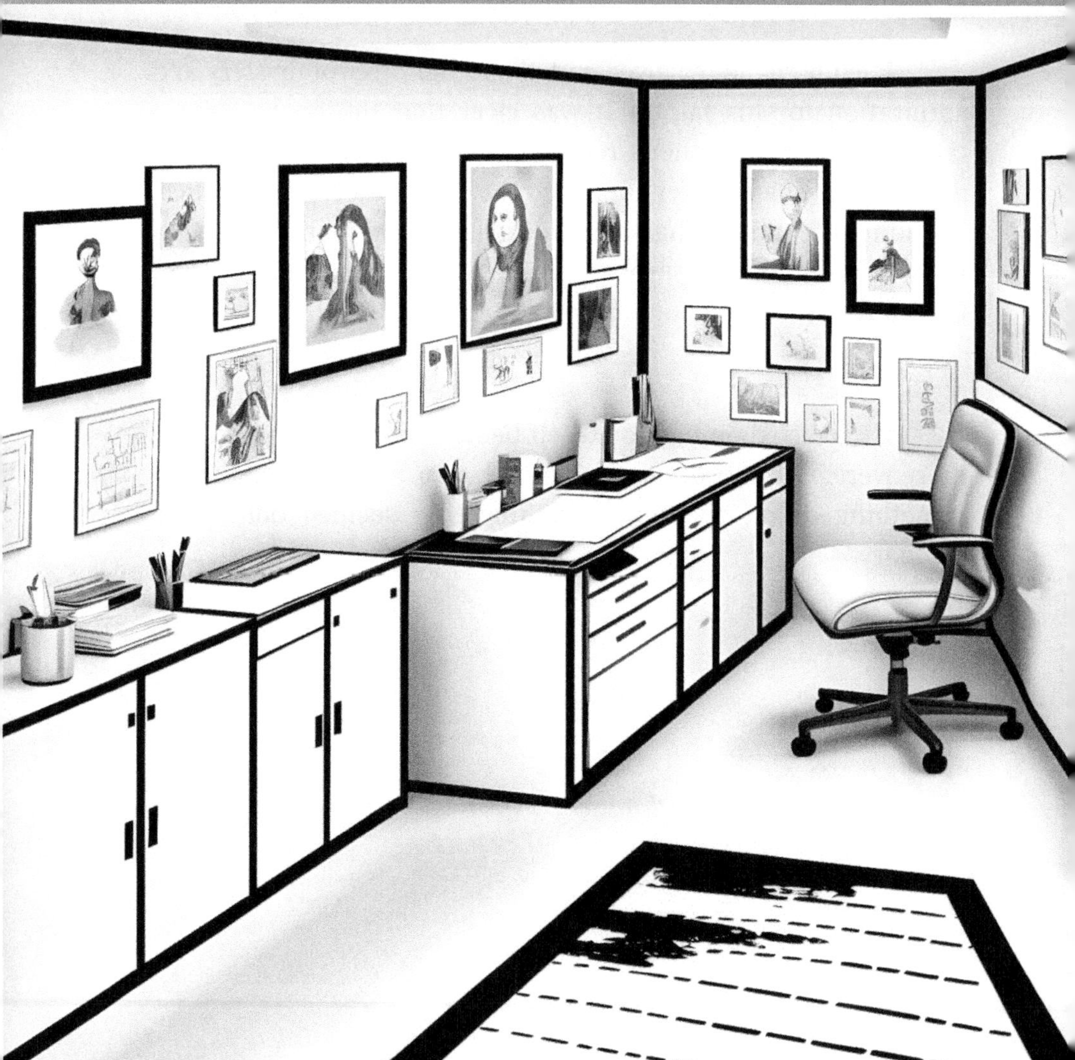

151
11
59
97
31
109
29
73
127
106
79
23
193
43
113
7
61
67
71
13
41
19
53
89
37
5
17
199
47
3
109

HOTEL ROOM RIDDLE

Shocking Revelations

David, after identifying the room he thought had been his father's, made his way to the hotel's front desk. The atmosphere was calm, with friendly and attentive staff. He checked in, providing his personal information and explaining that he wanted a specific room. The receptionist, upon checking availability, informed him that the room was occupied by a long-stay guest.

While checking in, the clerk made a casual observation that immediately caught David's attention. He mentioned that the coincidence in their last names was curious, noting that the long-term guest in that particular room shared the same last name as David.

With his heart beating faster, he asked directly if the guest's name was that of his father. As his suspicions were confirmed, he quickly explained to the clerk that his father had recently passed away. He shared that he was following in his father's final footsteps, a personal journey that had led him to that hotel in Wanaka.

The receptionist listened attentively and sympathetically to David's story. The revelation that the guest was his father and that he had recently passed away seemed to affect him. After a few moments of silence, the clerk agreed to give him the room keys. He offered his condolences and assured him that any outstanding expenses for his father's stay would be covered by him.

He thanked the receptionist and took the keys with a mixture of nervousness and anticipation. He knew that entering the room would be a significant step in his quest, a direct connection to his father's final days. With keys in hand, he headed down the hallway, each step bringing him closer to an unknown chapter in his father's life, one that he hoped would shed light on the mysteries he had been pursuing.

With the keys trembling slightly in his hand, he opened the door to the room where his father had spent his last days. The room was spotless, evidence of the recent passage of the cleaning service. It was a large space, flooded with natural light, with views overlooking a calm and serene landscape. The large bed, a built-in closet, a full bathroom and a small office in one corner formed the setting where the last chapters of her father's life had unfolded.

He walked into the room, each object he saw capturing his attention. The closet contained some clothes, recognizable as his father's. They were enough for about four days, meticulously ordered and cared for. They were enough for about four days, meticulously ordered and cared for. The style and markings were unmistakable, evoking memories of shared moments.

The bathroom, though small, was equipped with everything he needed. On the countertop, he found his father's signature cologne and a box for glasses, personal items that lent a sense of closeness and familiarity to the room.

But it was in the small office that he felt the most intense connection with his father. On the table, neatly arranged, were several objects that immediately captured his interest. An old newspaper, a journal, similar to the ones his father used to carry on his travels and expeditions, lay open, as if waiting to be read. Next to it, an open letter and an object that appeared to be a talisman.

He approached the table and reverently picked up the journal. As he flipped through its pages, he realized that it contained notes, reflections and sketches from his father, an intimate record of his thoughts and discoveries during his time in New Zealand. The open letter, in a handwriting unfamiliar to David, seemed to be an important piece in the puzzle he was piecing together. And the talisman, an enigmatic and possibly significant object, suggested a depth to his father's research that he was just beginning to understand.

The room, in its serene normality, was a contrast to the whirlwind of emotions and questions flooding David's mind. Every object, every detail, was a clue, a fragment of the larger story he was trying to decipher. With the journal, the letter and the talisman in hand, he felt he was closer to understanding not only the mysteries surrounding his father's life and work, but also the legacy he had left him.

Sitting in the quiet hotel room, he took a closer look at his father's diary with a mixture of respect and curiosity. He soon realized that this journal was devoted exclusively to his father's last trip to New Zealand. The pages were filled with meticulous entries, personal reflections and a series of detailed drawings.

As he turned the pages, he found several sketches made by his father of jade stones, each with distinct and unique shapes. These drawings were accompanied by notes that revealed his father's interest in these objects, although the specific purpose behind this interest was unclear. In addition, there was a small sketch of a map, but the details were too vague to identify a precise location.

What intrigued most were several icons scattered throughout the diary, symbols he did not recognize that seemed to have special meaning. Alongside these icons, his father had left a record of his daily activities, providing a chronological view of his last days.

He then focused on the open letter he had found next to the diary. The message was from days before his father's death and had been written by someone named Dr. Keleby. The contents of the letter were surprising: Dr. Keleby mentioned having found a new clue related to James Cook's treasure, a subject that had apparently occupied much of his father's final research.

The mention of Cook's treasure immediately captured David's attention. He knew that Cook had been a famous explorer and that any reference to treasure linked to him could be of great importance. The possibility that his father was on the trail of a historic discovery added another layer of mystery and urgency to his search.

With the letter in hand, he immersed himself in his reading, seeking to understand the relationship between Dr. Keleby, the Cook treasure and his father's final days. Each word seemed to be a crucial piece of the puzzle, a vital connection in the web of mysteries he was unraveling. The letter not only offered clues to the purpose of his father's trip to New Zealand, but also opened the door to new questions and possibilities that he was eager to explore.

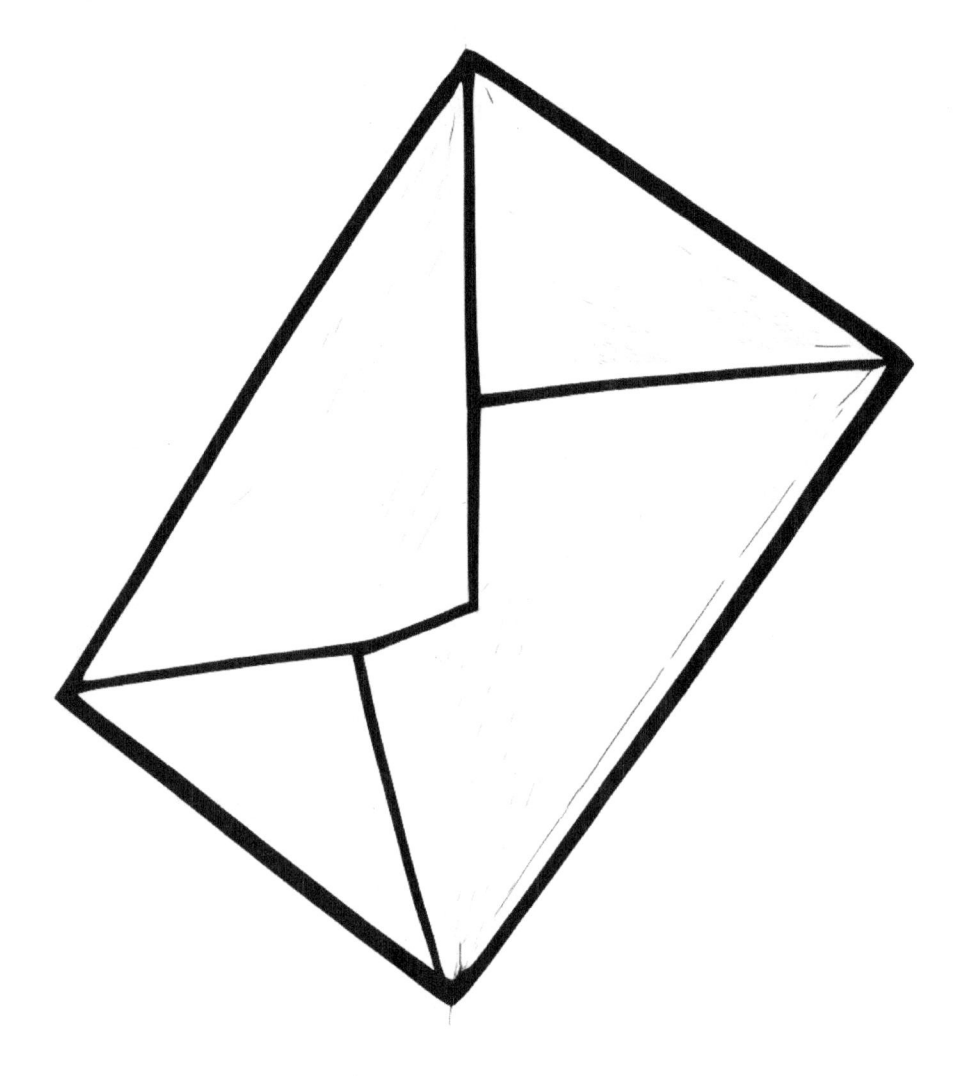

Dear Friend,

I hope this letter finds you enjoying the peace and quiet you love so much. I am writing from New Zealand, surrounded by its splendid scenery and filled with an enthusiasm that I cannot wait to share with you.

You see, my dear friend, my tireless search has borne sweeter fruit than I ever imagined. After years of tracing the story of the celebrated James Cook, I have found something that could change everything. Remember those long debates about Cook's voyage to New Zealand in 1769? We always wondered if he left more than footprints and maps. Well, it looks like our speculation might have some truth to it.

Recently, in a small, forgotten antique store, I came across a map and talisman that I'm sure date from Cook's time. The map is worn and battered, but one can still discern lines and markings that suggest hidden treasure. And the talisman, with its ancient engravings, seems to be a crucial piece of the puzzle.

I know it may sound like the plot of one of those adventure novels we loved so much when we were young, but I assure you, this is real. I can't help but recall our talks about Cook's adventurous spirit, his meticulous documentation of the islands and his interaction with the Maori tribes. This discovery could be a lost testimony of those historic moments.

Now, my friend, I am writing to you not only to share this exciting news, but also to ask you to come to New Zealand. Your experience and knowledge would be invaluable in this adventure. Together, we could unravel the mystery of this forgotten treasure and immerse ourselves in a part of history still waiting to be told. Despite being old and bald, my eyesight doesn't fail me!!! I now wear a beard, hehehe!

I look forward to your response and the possibility of meeting again, not only as friends, but as companions in a quest that could be the culmination of our careers and dreams.

With affection and excitement,

                Dr. Keleby

DIARY

New Zeland

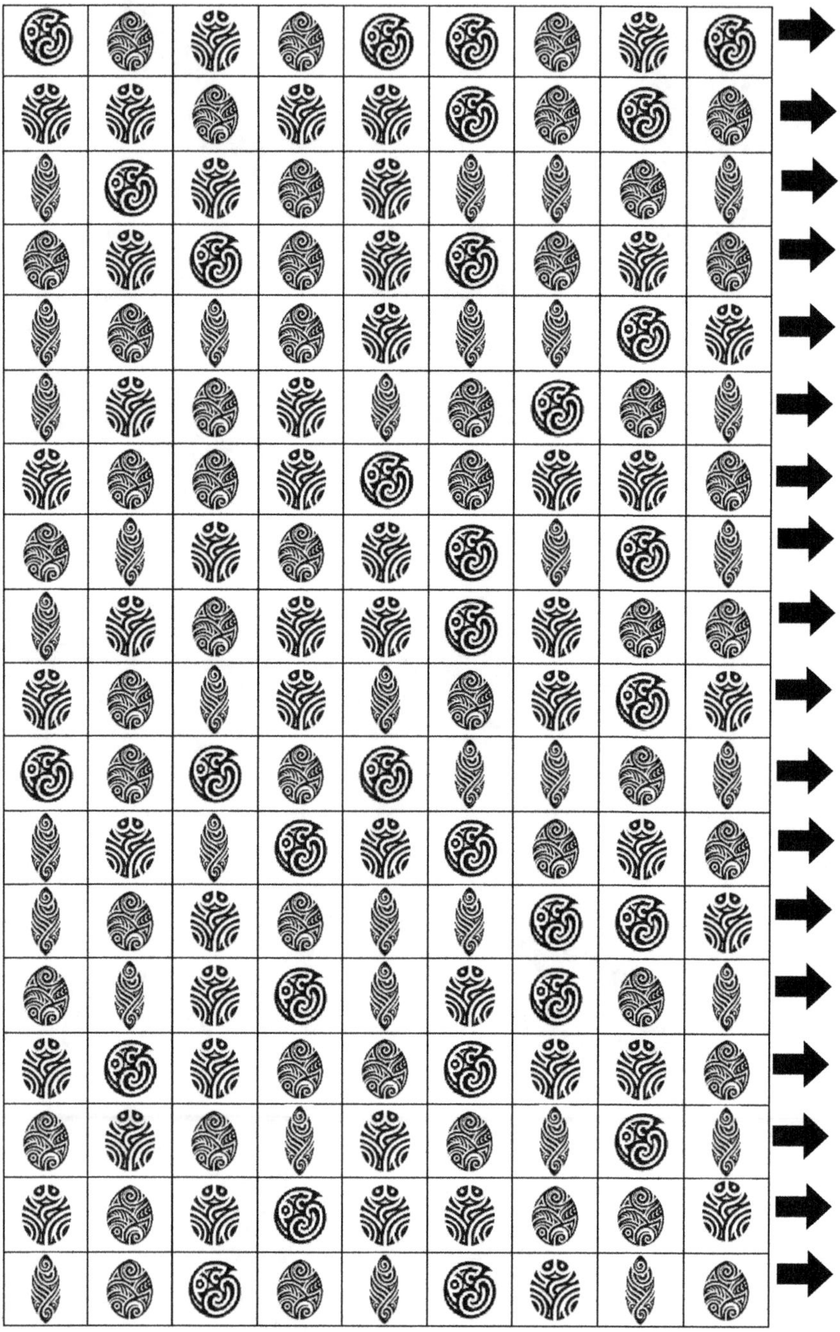

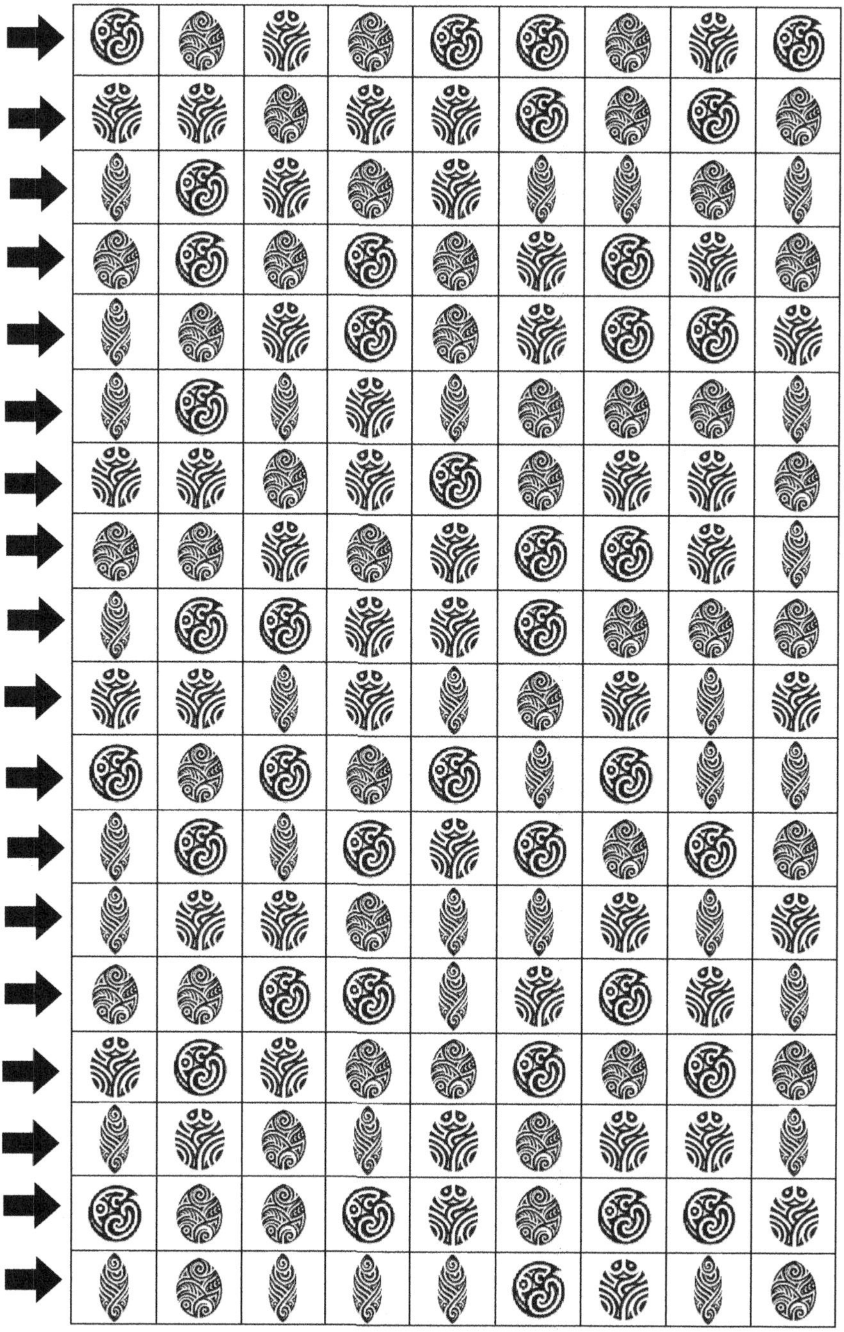

FRIDGE RIDDLE

An Unexpected Journey

The grid of letters and symbols found on the refrigerator had been a challenging puzzle, but David managed to decipher the hidden message. The words revealed pointed to a new destination, a new phase in the quest that had begun in his father's office. Although he wasn't clear on the exact place he needed to go or the motive behind this new clue, he knew it was a necessary step in unraveling the mystery his father had left him.

He pondered the questions that arose in his mind. "Why did you leave me all these clues, Dad? What do you expect me to find at the end of this path? And why are you warning me of danger?" Although the answers were still elusive, each discovery had brought him closer to understanding his father's riddles.

He headed for the garage, just as the last decoded message indicated. The garage door opened with difficulty and creaked open, revealing a large, but surprisingly empty and silent space. Daylight shyly streamed in through the dusty windows, illuminating the interior that seemed to have remained untouched for years.

The air in the garage was stagnant, with a smell of time and forgetfulness. He noticed that many of the objects were covered with protective plastic, now covered in a layer of dust that suggested years of neglect. He wondered how long it would have been since his father last used this space to prepare for his expeditions.

Among the objects not covered, a few items stood out that seemed to have been an integral part of her father's adventures: an old bicycle with flat tires, testimony to the effects of time; an empty cage that let the imagination run wild as to what or who might have inhabited it; and a spear with a spearhead of strange green material, possibly a relic of some expedition to distant lands.

Here his father's memories and echoes of his past expeditions were kept. The garage was filled with tools, maps, and various objects his father had used in his research. Each one of them was a testimony of a life dedicated to the investigation of secrets.

In the garage, he began to look for any clues that might give him a clue to his next destination. He went through old maps and notes his father had left behind, looking for some connection to the decoded message. Among the objects, he found a series of photographs of faraway and exotic places, notes on travel routes, and a field journal that his father used to keep on his expeditions.

David spent hours going through every object, every document, searching for the key that would tell him where he should go. The feeling that he was following in his father's footsteps, that he was living a kind of echo of his adventures, was overwhelming. He felt as if he were walking in a shadow that stretched across time, connecting him to his father in a way he had never experienced before.

What caught his attention most, however, was a slate filled with scribbles and notes. He walked over to examine it, discovering that it was covered with drawings, formulas and words that seemed to form a mental map of her father's thoughts and plans. Some of the scribbles were rudimentary maps, others appeared to be calculations or lists of equipment needed for travel.

He ran his fingers over the strokes on the board, trying to connect the scribbles to what he had learned so far. Each item in the garage, from the bicycle to the spear, seemed to tell a part of his father's story, a chapter in a book that David was eager to read and understand in its entirety.

As he explored the room, he felt the pieces of the puzzle begin to fit together. Each object, each note, was a clue that helped him piece together his father's routes and expeditions. It was clear that, in order to follow in his father's footsteps and discover the secrets he had left behind, he would have to immerse himself further into the world of exploration and discovery that had defined his life.

With a renewed sense of purpose, he continued his exploration of every nook and cranny of that room, determined to follow every clue and decipher every hidden message, knowing that each discovery brought him one step closer to the truth he sought.

Immersed in the gloom, he was poring over the scribble-strewn blackboard. Initially, he had thought of them as mere drawings or random notes, but, reflecting on the meticulousness with which his father approached everything in his life, he began to see them in a different light. "Nothing you did was without purpose, was it, Dad?" he murmured.

He realized that every image, every line and every shape on the board, must be part of a larger puzzle, a puzzle that his father had meticulously created. The idea that his father, a man of precise methods and reasoning, would have left anything to chance was unthinkable. Every stroke had to have a reason for being.

David spent hours in front of the blackboard, analyzing every detail. The symbols began to take a new shape in his mind, they were no longer simple sketches, but parts of a map, a set of instructions or perhaps coordinates to a specific location. "Is this a map to an unknown destination?" he wondered, trying to decipher the meaning hidden in the markings.

He contemplated the scribbles on the board, each symbol becoming a piece of a puzzle he was eager to complete. The possibility that those traces were a map to a remote location was becoming more and more plausible. He remembered his father's stories, replete with adventures in exotic and unknown places, and couldn't help but wonder, "Is it possible that one of those places is my destination?" He felt a mixture of excitement and apprehension at the thought of what he might find in that essential quest, a journey that would take him beyond the known.

With the conviction that he was about to discover a crucial location in his father's research, he prepared for the next stage of his journey. Armed with notes, maps and unwavering determination, he was ready to follow the trail that the signs on the board pointed him to, a trail that would lead him to unravel one of the greatest mysteries in his father's life.

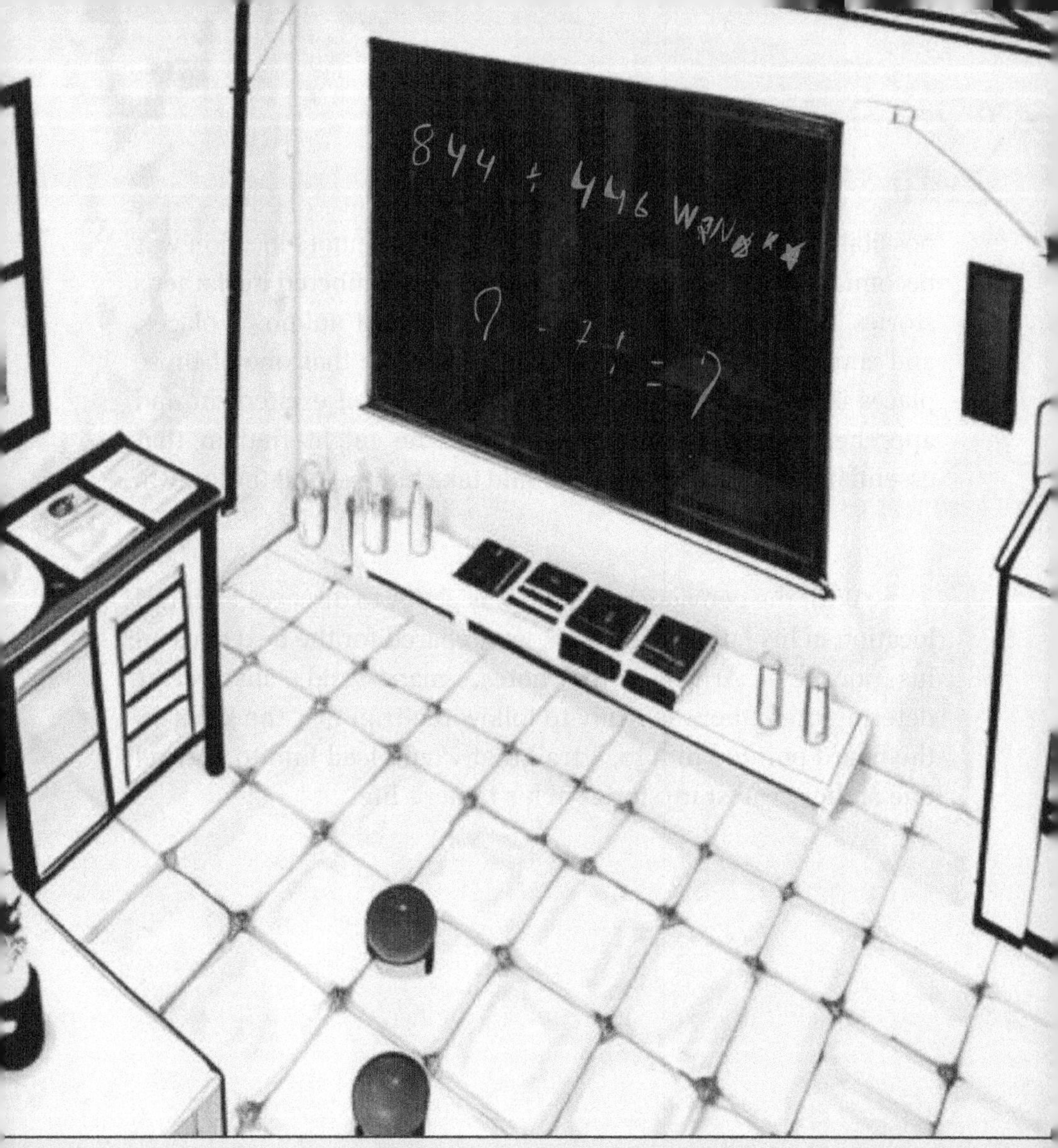
844 ÷ 446

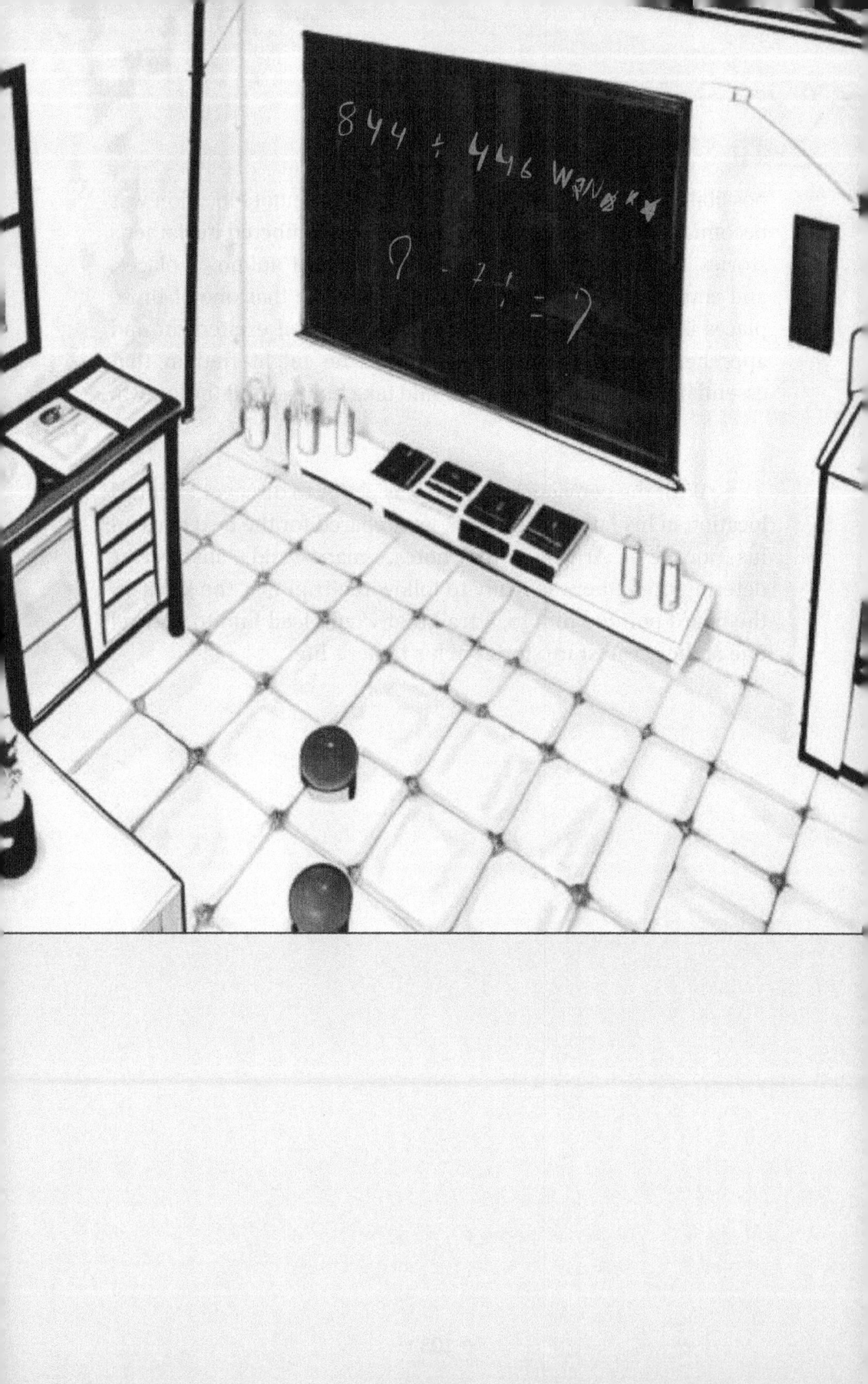

844p + 446   W*N*K*

🔲 - 71 = ??

PUZZLE BOOKSHELF BOOKS

The Hidden Room

David, stopped at a book that seemed to be slightly out of tune with the others on the shelf. It was an old tome, with a worn leather cover and a spine that showed more signs of use than the books around it. Intrigued, he carefully removed it from its place, feeling an unexpected weight in his hands.

When he opened it, he discovered that it was no ordinary book. The pages had been scrupulously trimmed to form a hollow, inside of which rested a metal lever with strange engravings. David's surprise quickly turned to curiosity. "What is this, Dad, a key to something else?" he wondered aloud.

As he examined the shelf more closely, he noticed a subtle mark where the book had been. Following an impulse, he inserted the lever into a small, almost invisible opening in the wood. With a firm twist, he heard a click and, to his amazement, the entire shelf began to move slowly, revealing a secret room that had been hidden behind it.

His heart was racing as he crossed the threshold into the unknown room. The room was illuminated by a dim light emanating from a lamp, creating dancing shadows on the walls. His gaze was immediately drawn to a table in the center of the room, on which lay a notebook with a meticulously written list of various plants, each accompanied by detailed notes and drawings.

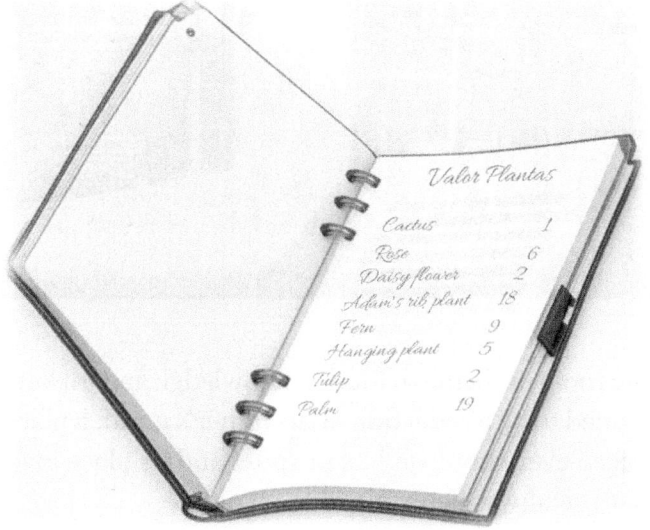

Valor Plantas

Cactus	1
Rose	6
Daisy flower	2
Adam's rib plant	18
Fern	9
Hanging plant	5
Tulip	2
Palm	19

However, what really caught his attention was the wall opposite the entrance. It was covered with an intricate array of gears and mechanisms, like the inside of a gigantic clock or a complex machine from a bygone era. David approached, fascinated by the design and precision of the components.

"I have no idea what to do with this," he admitted quietly, touching one of the gears gingerly. It seemed clear that the gears were part of some sort of puzzle or mechanism that needed to be solved, but how and why remained a mystery.

The room, a shrine of hidden knowledge and unsolved mysteries, seemed to be a reflection of his father's mind: a place where every object, every note, had its purpose and its place in a larger puzzle that David was determined to complete.

What would happen if those gears were moved? David wondered quietly.

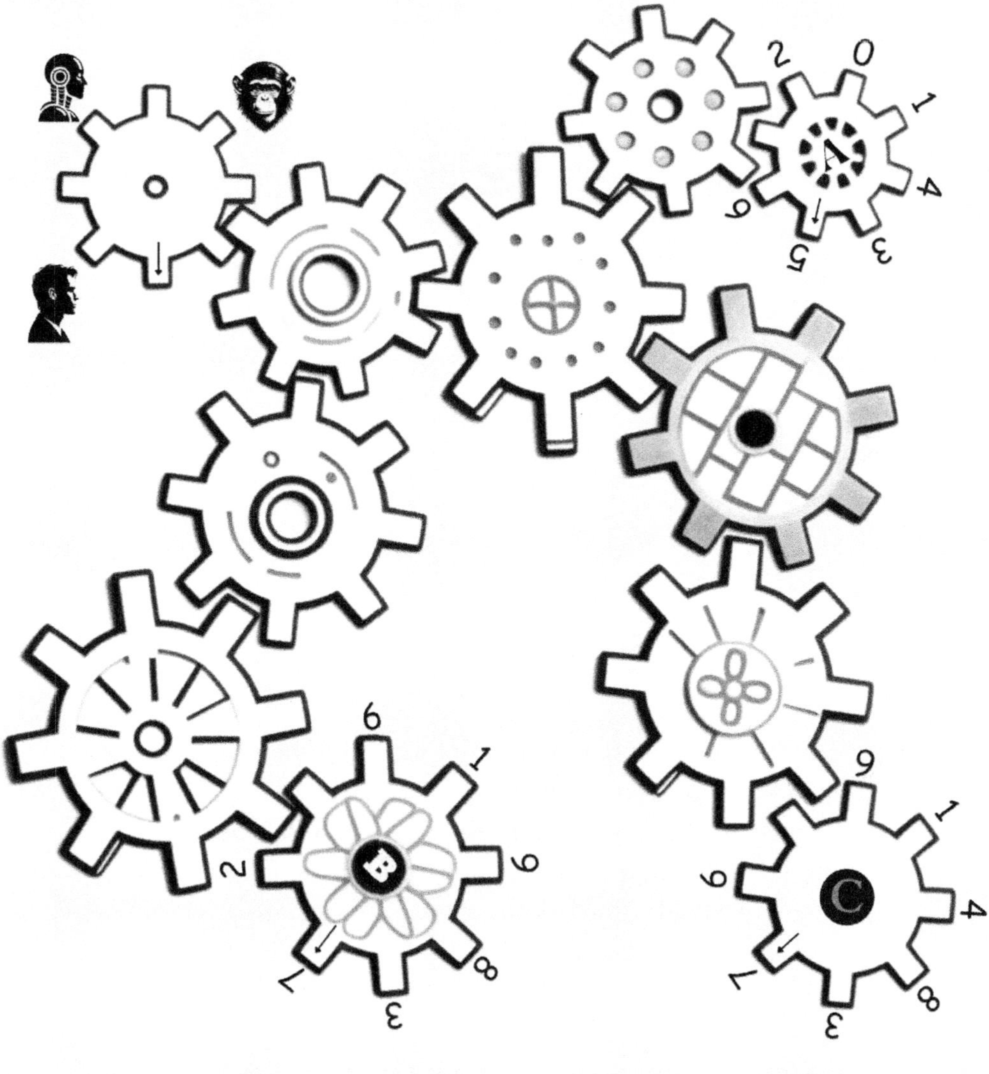
A
B
C

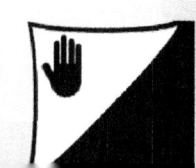

CAVE RIDDLE

The Fate of Secrets

After a thorough exploration guided by the talisman and the diary, he arrived at the exact spot marked on the map. In the heart of the grotto, illuminated by the weak beam of his flashlight, he found what seemed to be the end of his long journey: a small, half-open chest, hidden in a carefully concealed niche in the cave wall.

With his heart pounding in his chest, he approached the chest. Opening it fully, his eyes were met with a collection of antiques, precious metal objects whose luster still lingered despite the passage of time. There, in the stillness of the grotto, he realized that he had found what his father had sought for so long, the lost treasure that had consumed the last years of his life.

"How would you feel, Dad, knowing we've made it?" he wondered aloud, as he contemplated the contents of the chest. He felt a mixture of pride, excitement and a deep sense of connection with her father. It was as if, across time and space, they shared that moment of triumph and discovery.

Looking at the relics before him, David questioned himself about the future. What should he do with this treasure now? The responsibility for that decision weighed on him. Should he turn it over to the authorities, making sure it became part of the historical and cultural heritage, or should he keep it as a personal memento of his father's testimony and passion?

Moreover, this discovery could mark the beginning of a new chapter in his life. Until that moment, he had lived in the shadow of his father, a translator of dead languages, but this adventure had transformed him. He had followed a path full of mysteries and dangers, proving to be much more than a scholar. This treasure, and all it represented, could be the beginning of a new life, a life of exploration and discovery.

With the chest in his hands, he felt at a threshold, not only physical, but also emotional and existential. The search was over, but at the same time, a new journey was beginning. With a sense of respect for the past and anticipation for the future, he would have to make a decision about what to do with the chest, a decision that would mark his own path in life.

With the chest firmly clutched in his hands, he paused for a moment to examine its contents in more detail. The pieces lying within were exquisite, each one meticulously carved and adorned with inlaid gemstones. They appeared to be relics of the island's indigenous tribes, each object telling its own story, a narrative of a rich and mysterious past that had become intertwined with the present.

The weight of the chest was considerable, not only physically, but also in terms of its historical and personal significance. He understood that he had to handle it with the utmost care and respect. He began the slow and cautious trek back through the grotto, carrying with him the treasure he had so determinedly sought.

Walking in the opposite direction through the cave, David's every step was imbued with a new perception of his surroundings and himself. The light filtering through the cave's entrance hole was projected like a laser beam, marking the path back to the outside world. Reaching the hole, he carefully placed the chest on the ground and pushed it out, making sure it was safe.

Then, using the rock he had previously placed as a support, he climbed towards the exit. As he emerged from the grotto and felt the fresh, pure air on his face, he was filled with a deep relief. The atmosphere in the cave had been oppressive, charged with mystery and antiquity, and now, back outside, he felt liberated and renewed.

Looking up at the open sky, he reflected on his journey. The experience of discovering the chest and what it contained had changed his perspective. He no longer saw the world as just a scholar or a translator of ancient texts, but as someone who had touched a living part of history, someone who had connected with his father's legacy in a way he had never imagined.

With the chest safely outside the cave, he knew he faced new decisions and responsibilities. What to do with these relics? How to share this discovery in a way that respected both his cultural background and his father's legacy? These questions would accompany him on his way back, but for now, he allowed himself a moment to simply breathe and appreciate the magnitude of what he had accomplished.

With the treasure chest secured and daylight beginning to fade, David began his return to the vehicle that would take him back to civilization. As he walked, deep reflection accompanied him, marked by the realization of how much he had changed throughout this unexpected adventure. He felt different, he was not the person who had started this journey; now, he was an explorer, a discoverer of secrets, a continuator of his father's legacy.

"This is more than I ever imagined for myself," he thought. He had crossed the world in search of answers, and he had found them. He had completed the work his father had begun, feeling at peace and in harmony with himself. The treasure he had discovered, previously unknown relics, represented not only a significant archaeological find, but also a personal and intimate connection to his father.

With each step toward the vehicle, David felt the adrenaline of discovery transform into a new energy, a motivation to keep going. "I can do more, I can follow in your footsteps and still forge my own path," he reflected. This trip had ignited in him a desire to undertake his own research, to continue exploring the mysteries of the past.

However, a nagging question echoed in his mind: what to do with the treasure? On the one hand, it was the fruit of his effort and discovery, something that no one else knew existed. On the other hand, he was aware of its historical and cultural value, belonging to the people who once inhabited those lands, a piece of living history.

"This treasure...is not mine alone. It's part of a bigger story, one that belongs to the world," he told himself. The decision was not easy. What was the right thing to do? He considered working with institutions and experts to make sure the treasure was preserved, studied and shared in a way that respected its historical and cultural significance.

Arriving at the vehicle, with the chest at his side, David looked to the horizon, feeling full of purpose and direction. He was ready to face the challenges ahead, certain that every step he took was a tribute to his father's legacy and the beginning of his own journey as an explorer and keeper of the secrets of the past.

DO I KEEP THE TREASURE?

YOU DO **NOT** KEEP THE TREASURE

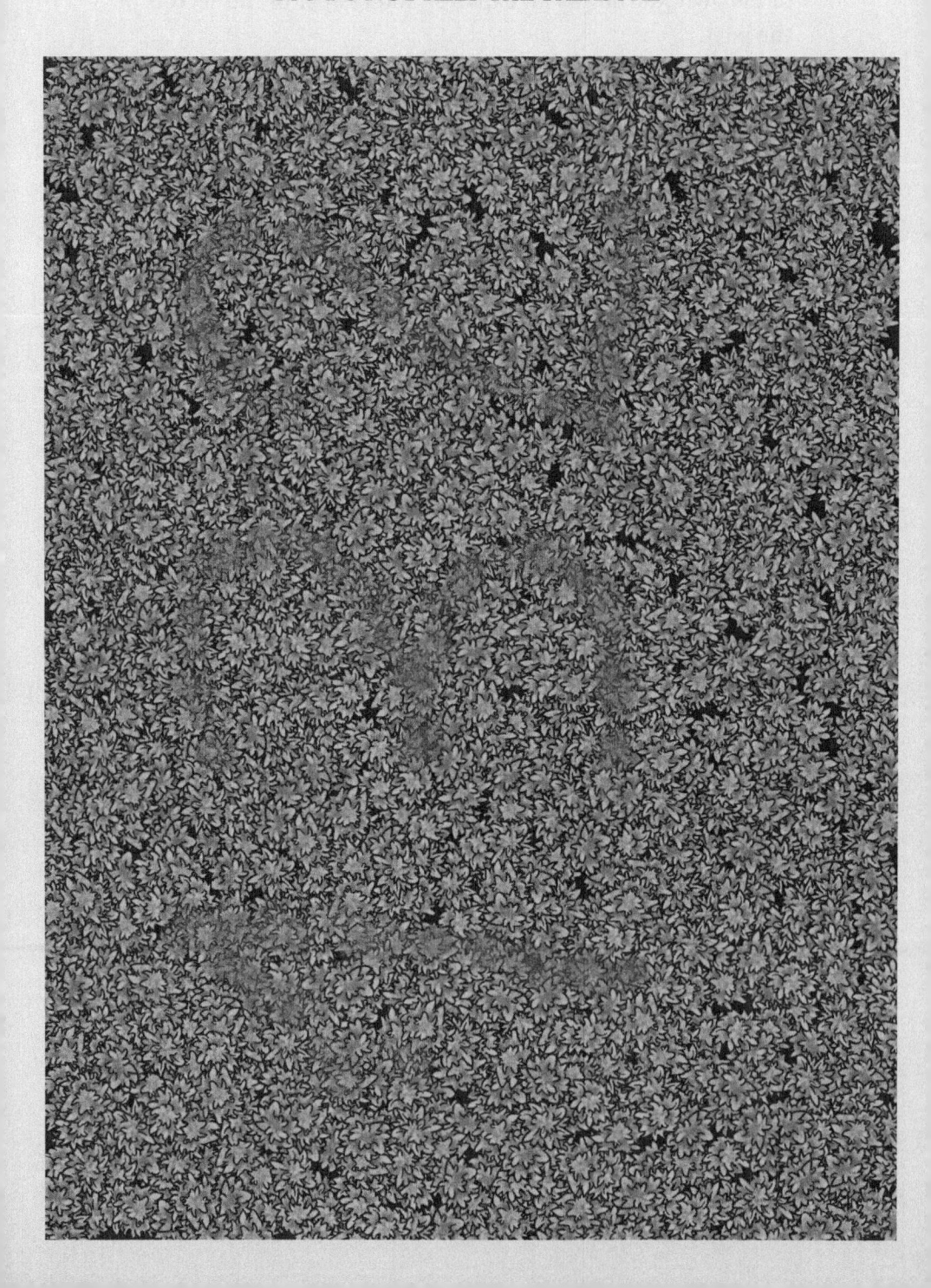

YOU KEEP THE TREASURE

RIDDLE BOX OFFICE

Clues at Home

The discovery of the floor plan hidden in the back of the quirky canvas had been eye-opening for David. Upon close examination, he realized that it was a detailed floor plan of his childhood home, the same house where he had lived with his father for over 25 years. It was a meticulous representation of every room, every hallway and every nook and cranny, including some details he had never noticed before.

****

David without wasting time went to his childhood home, he had memories of his childhood, good and not so pleasant memories of those 4 walls.

He now stood in front of his old house, observing it with a mixture of nostalgia and renewed curiosity. The structure, though familiar, seemed to hold secrets he had never perceived during his childhood and youth. The house, with its time-worn walls and windows reflecting the years of stories lived there, stood as a silent witness to his father's mysteries.

As he opened the door, a wave of memories washed over David. Every step inside the house was a step back in time. He remembered the days when his father would prepare for his expeditions, filling the house with an air of mystery and anticipation. He remembered how, with each trip, his father had grown more distant, becoming more and more immersed in his research until those trips became extended absences.

Now, with the floor plan in hand, he began to explore the house as if for the first time. He looked at each room through a new perspective, searching for clues that had gone unnoticed. The living room, where they used to spend evenings together; the dining room, the scene of quiet dinners; the kitchen, where they prepared succulent treats; and the garage, the place to amass our old memories.

He walked into his childhood bedroom, a space that seemed to have been frozen in time. The walls, adorned with posters of his childhood heroes and shelves full of books and toys, evoked endless memories. Each object reminded him of moments of joy, of childhood discoveries, but also of loneliness, especially in the years when his father's trips became more frequent and prolonged.

As he explored the room, he couldn't help but feel that the memories were intertwined with something else: the possibility that his father had left coded clues in the most familiar places. He began to examine every nook and cranny, every object he had grown up with, wondering if any of them might be more than they seemed.

He opened drawers and went through old notebooks, looking for some pattern or hidden message. He found drawings he had made as a child, stories written in his clumsy childish handwriting, but nothing to suggest a coded message. However, the feeling that something important was hidden among those memories persisted.

With a sigh, he left his room and headed for his father's room. As he entered, he was enveloped in an atmosphere of nostalgia and melancholy. The room was just as he remembered it: tidy, functional, with a large bed and a bedside table full of books and papers. Here, the memories were different, tinged by the long hours of solitude he had spent while his father was away.

He approached the bedside table, his attention focused on an object that, under any other circumstances, would not have caught his attention. It was an ordinary object, one he had seen countless times without giving it much thought. But now, with his new understanding of the secrets and enigmas surrounding his father's life, David couldn't help but wonder, "Is this also part of the mystery?"

He looked at the object, feeling the memories of his childhood mingle with the urgent need to decipher his father's secrets. That object, so ordinary and yet potentially so significant, became the focus of her curiosity. He wondered what secrets it might be hiding and how it could be related to his father's research and discoveries.

David found a familiar, yet unusual artifact: a flashlight. However, this was no ordinary flashlight, but one equipped with black light, a type of light often used to reveal hidden messages or details invisible to the naked eye. With a sense of anticipation, he turned on the flashlight and a beam of ultraviolet light cut through the darkness of the room.

He decided to use the flashlight to inspect the rest of the house, wondering if his father had used this technique to hide important information. He went through each room meticulously, running the ultraviolet light over walls, furniture and personal items, looking for any traces of hidden messages or symbols.

The search was exhaustive and, for a time, fruitless. More than half of the house had been inspected without discovering anything out of the ordinary. However, David was not discouraged. He continued his meticulous search, driven by the conviction that his father had left something for him, something that could only be revealed in the right light.

It was in the kitchen that his perseverance finally paid off. As he passed the flashlight in front of the refrigerator, covered almost completely by a collection of travel magnets and notes, he noticed a peculiar glow. Intrigued, he reached over and began removing the magnets one by one.

Beneath the layer of magnets, a grid was revealed with letters and symbols that were only visible under the black light. He felt a shudder as he realized that he was looking at another encrypted message, another enigma that his father had prepared for him.

He stood for a moment in silence, staring at the grid, trying to decipher its meaning. "What are you trying to tell me, Dad?" he wondered.

With the grid revealed, he knew he had a new mystery to solve, a new path to follow in his tireless quest. Armed with the black light flashlight and the newly discovered message, he prepared to continue unraveling the secrets his father had left scattered throughout his former home..

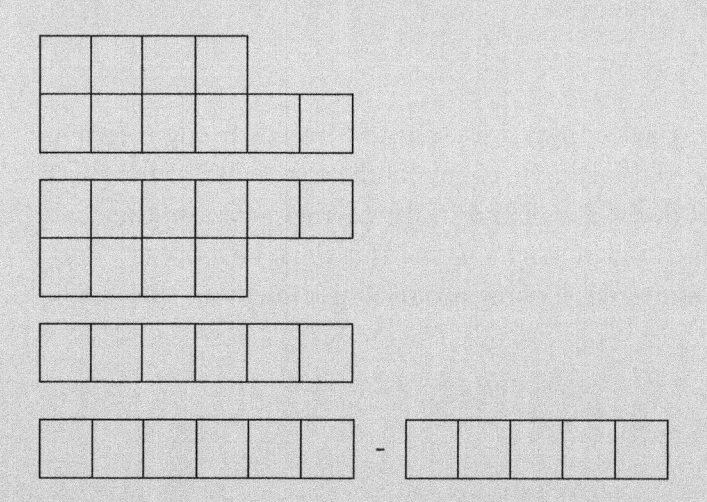

T	U	N	P	C	O	D	E	A	T	R	U
I	P	S	E	C	R	E	T	M	H	W	I
S	H	Z	S	P	R	A	N	W	G	T	S
M	Q	T	E	X	U	P	R	S	I	F	Ñ
H	W	G	F	G	J	K	R	Y	E	H	O
P	B	Z	R	Ñ	A	W	Q	B	A	X	T
Y	M	A	P	S	X	R	P	E	Y	Z	P
R	V	Z	G	L	F	T	A	U	T	T	B
R	Q	Y	B	Q	R	E	R	G	E	V	Q
U	H	E	W	Ñ	S	P	Q	T	N	S	U
Ñ	X	G	O	O	G	L	E	Z	I	Ñ	I
I	B	U	R	P	U	W	T	O	N	Y	W

RIDDLE GEARS WALL

The Detective's Trail

The secret room was plunged into darkness as the door automatically closed behind David, leaving him isolated in stony silence. For a moment, surprise and bewilderment gripped him. He took a deep breath, trying to calm his racing heartbeat and analyze the situation calmly.

"Think, David, think," he said to himself, trying to orient himself in the darkness. He remembered the sound of the gears moving and how, when placed in the correct position, they had activated some kind of mechanism. "This must be more evidence of Dad," he muttered, looking around for something that might help him.

> If at this point in the adventure you have managed to decipher the **BONUS** CHAPTER, you can go directly to **page 127**. If you have not yet done so, you can continue reading or try to decipher the extra chapter of the story".

In the room now closed and plunged into darkness, he felt momentarily overwhelmed by the situation. The urgency to find a way out compelled him to act. He began to feel the walls methodically, moving his hands over the cold surface in search of a switch or mechanism that might open the door.

He could find nothing that resembled a switch. The only noticeable feature were the gears he had previously interacted with to open the secret compartment, but they were now immobile, as if the mechanism had been locked after activation.

He returned to the door, examining it in more detail. He remembered outlines of the message, but it was not enough to decipher its full meaning. David concentrated, trying to remember every detail of the message he had glimpsed in those brief moments.

As he continued his frantic search for a switch or some hidden mechanism in the locked room, his feet stumbled over something unexpected on the floor. He bent down and felt for the object that had caused his stumble. It was a cord, thin and long, stretched across the floor. "How did I not see that before?" he wondered, wondering if that cord might be the key to getting out of that room.

Following the path of the cord by feel, he discovered that it stretched across the room and ended at one end that was firmly fastened to the wall. With a mixture of hope and doubt, he grabbed the cord and pulled it carefully. To his surprise, the cord offered no resistance; rather, it slipped smoothly into his hand, as if waiting to be activated.

The moment he pulled the cord completely out of its hook on the wall, something extraordinary happened: a series of ultraviolet lights suddenly flared up, bathing the room in a ghostly, bluish light. The walls, once plain and featureless, now revealed a new level of detail under the ultraviolet light. Hidden patterns, symbols and text began to emerge, creating a visual spectacle that took his breath away.

> **Read only if you have deciphered the CHAPTER BONUS**
>
> His fingers touched the flashlight he always carried with him, a small beam of hope in that moment of uncertainty. Switching it on, the light cut through the darkness, revealing the contours of the shadow-filled room.
>
> He turned the beam toward the door, looking for a way to open it or some clue as to what to do next.

"This changes everything," David murmured, his eyes roaming the walls covered with information that was previously hidden from view. The symbols on the door, once barely visible, now glowed clearly, revealing their true form and meaning. He realized that what he had discovered was not simply a message or a set of instructions, but a set of 2 ideas, one on each side of the now closed door.

With a renewed sense of purpose, he began to study the symbols and text on the closed door. It was clear that this room was the nucleus of something much larger, a hub of information and knowledge that would be crucial to continuing his father's work.

With the ultraviolet light revealing the secrets of the room, I knew I had the tools I needed to move forward. It was the doorway to a new chapter in the search for truth. With determination and a sense of deep connection to his father, he prepared to decipher the secrets that now lay before him.

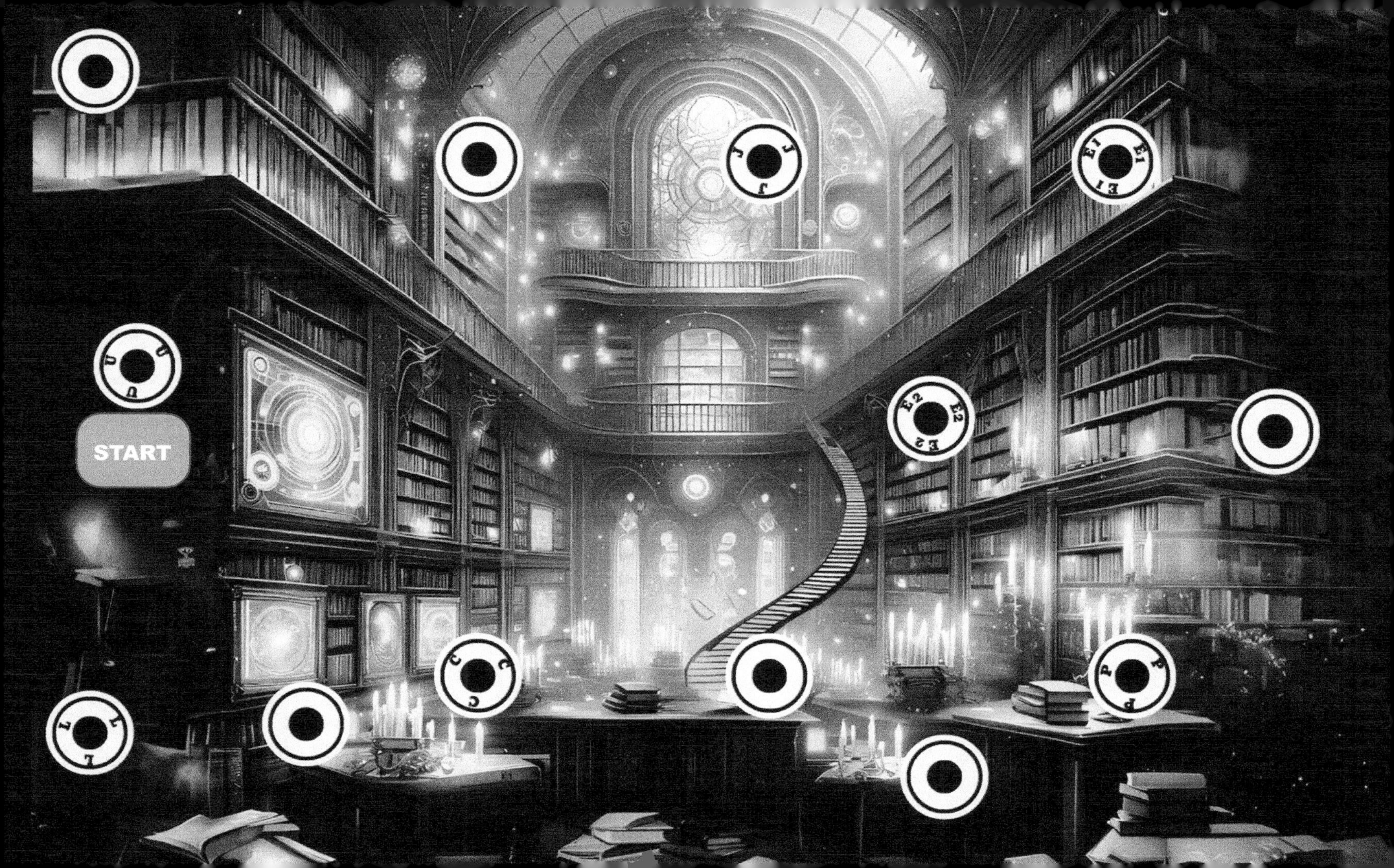
START
U U U
L L L
J J J
E1 E1 E1
E2 E2 E2
C C C
P P P

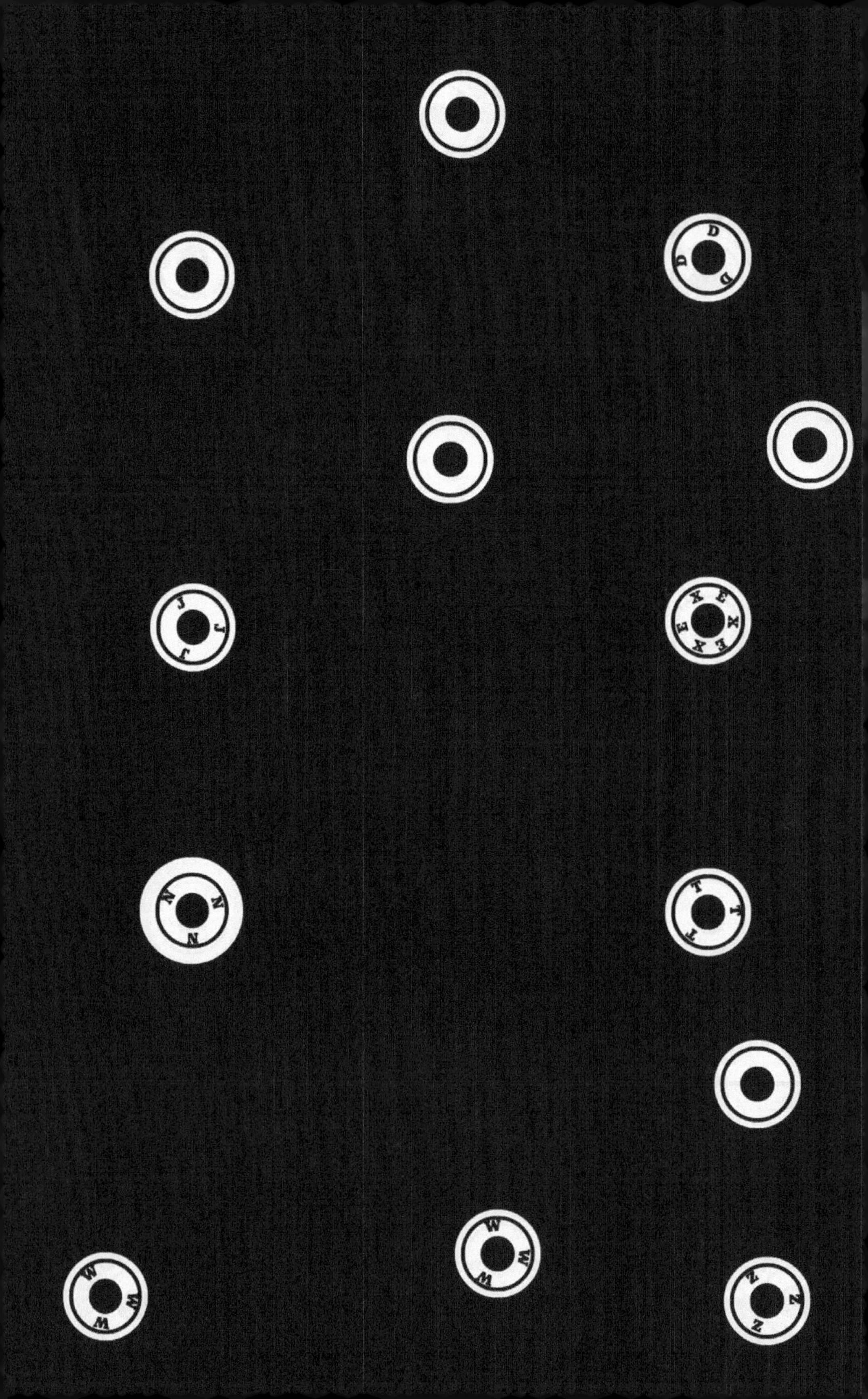
D D D
J J J
X E X E X E
N N N
T T T
W W W
W W W
Z Z Z

Maybe I need that cable that was on the floor?

You do NOT keep the treasure.

After his arduous and revealing adventure, David Mur was faced with a momentous decision. The treasure he had discovered, filled with relics and antiquities of New Zealand's Aboriginal people, represented a priceless historical and cultural legacy. After deep reflection, he made the decision not to keep the treasure for himself. Instead, he chose to donate it to New Zealand institutions, firmly believing that it belonged to the country's cultural heritage and should be shared and appreciated by all.

The donation was received with amazement and gratitude by the country's institutions. The relics and antiquities provided a rich new perspective on the history and culture of New Zealand's indigenous peoples. The decision not only strengthened the connection between the past and the present, but also opened doors for future research and discovery.

In recognition of his generosity and the significant impact of his donation, the institutions decided to rename an important part of the National Museum of New Zealand the "David Mur Rooms". This honor, more than a simple recognition, was a testament to the respect and admiration that David had earned in the country.

The "David Mur Rooms" became a space dedicated to the exhibition of relics found in the grotto, as well as other artifacts and elements of the country's Aboriginal history. The room was designed as a living tribute to the legacy of New Zealand's Aboriginal peoples and to David's contribution to the preservation and dissemination of their history.

Page 136

You keep the treasure.

After his journey full of discoveries and revelations, David Mur found himself at a crossroads. The treasure he had discovered, a collection of relics and antiquities of incalculable historical and cultural value, represented not only the legacy of the original peoples of New Zealand, but also the legacy of his own father. After deep reflection, David decided to take the treasure with him, with the firm intention of sharing these treasures with the world in a unique and meaningful way.

Back home, driven by a sense of stewardship and teaching, David conceived the idea of creating a permanent exhibit. This exhibit would not only house the newly discovered relics, but would also include other finds and objects from his father's expeditions. His vision was to create a space where people could learn, marvel and appreciate the cultural and historical riches of past civilizations.

With this goal in mind, David began working tirelessly on the project. He searched for the perfect location for the exhibition, preferring a setting that would resonate with the importance and majesty of the artifacts. He selected a historic building, bringing his own personal touch to the design and organization of the space. The exhibition would be a tribute to the people whose stories were inscribed on each piece and, at the same time, a tribute to the life of her father, a man who dedicated his existence to exploration and discovery.

Page 136

THANK YOU FOR CHOOSING THIS BOOK!

Before I say goodbye to the adventure, let me ask you a small request, could you leave me a review on the platform? Posting a review is the easiest way to support simple projects like this one.

Your opinion will help me to keep writing books. Help me to keep improving.

I leave you the QR code and the link so you can post a review.

AMAZON.COM

AMAZON.UK

If you want to solve a last enigma or receive information about new books or riddles, click here.

https://escaperiddle.com/unete-comunidad-inlges

TRAKS

Page 15

A: Complete the sudoku

B: Fill in all the boxes if a box is black it will be the same if there is another black box.

Page 21

A: It's interesting the composition of this painting, isn't it? Where have I seen those elements before?

B: In previous chapters you seem to comment something about "hats", "spiders" and some image of "pots".

Page 27

A: It's a game of Who's Who. Do we know anything about what Dr. Keleby looks like?

B: Discard people who do not match the physical characteristics described on the chart found in the hotel room.

Page 35

A: It is a room in New Zealand in the southern hemisphere.

B: Maybe you're looking at the doors from the wrong perspective.

Page 43

A: Does it appear to be simple "zeros", or is there more to it?

B: Find the number hidden between the zeros on each page to form a new number.

Page 47

A: Where have you seen that grid before, maybe it was filled in.

B: The order of the symbols in the chapter must be logical.

Page 51-55

A: In order for those holes to be holes, they will have to be cut out.

B: Is there anything on that sheet of newspaper that might overlap?

Page 63

A: Enter the QR by scanning the image.

B: Always keep in mind where North is.

C: Go to the chest at the end of the cave.

Page 69

A: It looks like a puzzle...

B: Arrange the cut pieces in order. It is easiest to start with the frames and follow the lines of the same color.

Page 77

A: It is a mathematical operation with Roman numerals.

B: With only the movement of a single bone, the operation must be correct. Which bone is it?

Page 85

A: It is interesting that all the numbers have a pattern but one.

B: ¡prime!

Page 97

A: Take a good look at the letter, its lines, colors or design.

B: Look at the chart in perspective. Don't let the tree keep you from seeing the forest.

Page 105

A: Did you find words on the fridge that you haven't used?

B: Find the location and you will find the number on the facade.

Page 109

A: You have to visualize what you have to rotate the gears with an order. The images represent the "evolution".

B: A, represents the past. B the present and C the future. Count the teeth of the gears as far as you need and the direction. Make sure that each gear moves in the direction that pushes the previous one.

Page 116-117

A: What can be seen between the trees?

B: Visualize that it can be glimpsed.

Page 123

A: It looks like a regular alphabet soup. Find the words and write them at the bottom.

B: Be careful as there are words that match a number of letters. They have to be related to each other.

Page 131

A: It's interesting that the image that comes out is somewhere else in the book. Perhaps a keyword appears there.

B: Those portholes would have to be pierced. And follow letter by letter a word.

C: The word you are looking for is in the title of the book.

SOLUTIONS

Page 15

[7][3] − [3][7] = 36

Page 21

55 spiders + 47 Hats + 16 pots= **118**

Page 27

Men + bald + without glasses + beard

44

Page 35

Number 87

Page 43

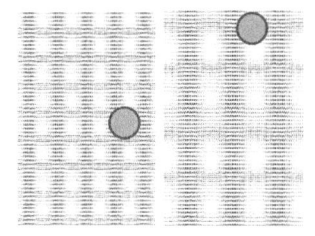

Number 48

Pag 47

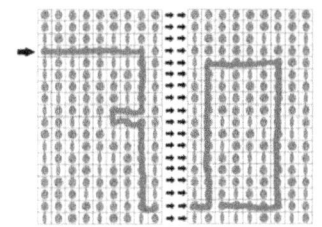

Number 70

Pag 51-55

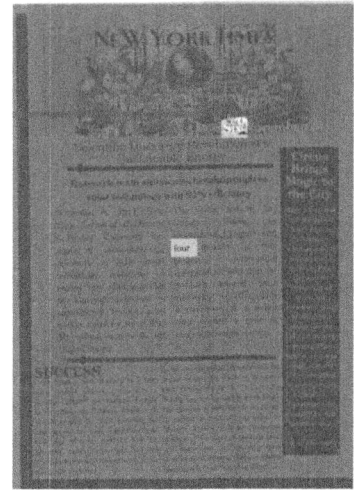

Number 64

Page 63

North – North – North – West – West – South – West – South.

Solution: **110**

Page 68-69

Number 80

Page 77

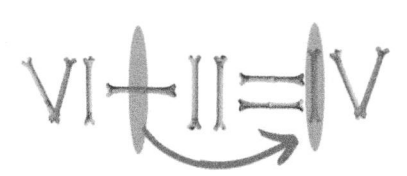

VI + II = IV

Number 56

Page 85

The number that does not match the rest is the only one that is not odd.

The number **106.**

You can also find the number since all numbers are prime numbers except 106.

Page 97

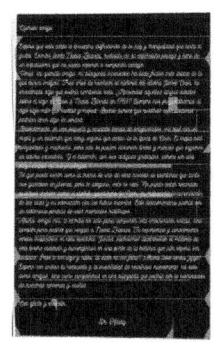

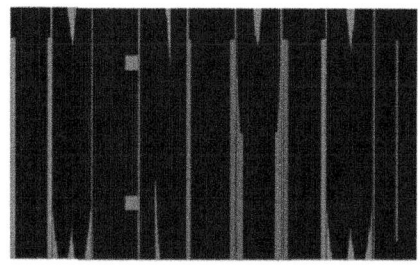

Number 22

Page 105

Replace the stars with "A" (clue given in the image of the refrigerator). Search Google Maps for the code, look at the facade of the building (99) and subtract 71.

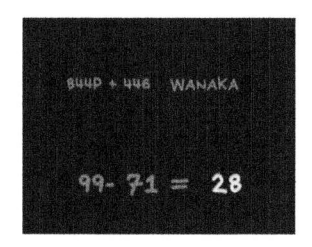

Page 109

Number 124

Page 116-117

Number 132

Number 134

Page 123

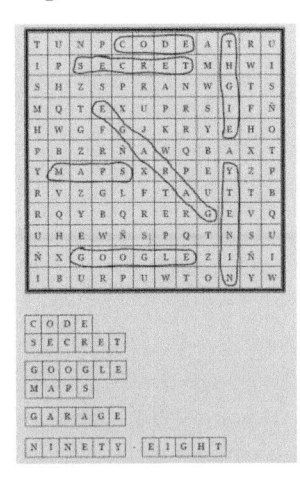

Number 98

~ 146 ~

Page 131

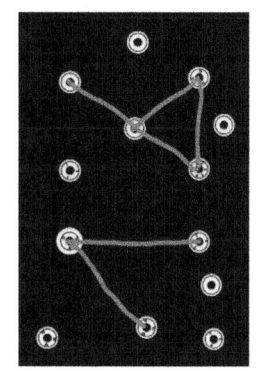

Number 16

NOTES

NOTES

NOTES

Printed in Great Britain
by Amazon